JOHN DARLING

JOHN DARLING

An Australian Filmmaker in Bali

Edited by
Graeme MacRae and Anton Lucas

Published in conjunction with Monash University's
Herb Feith Indonesian Engagement Centre

Monash University Publishing
Matheson Library Annexe
40 Exhibition Walk
Monash University
Clayton, Victoria 3800, Australia
publishing.monash.edu/

Monash University Publishing: the discussion starts here

© Copyright 2022
Copyright of this collection in its entirety is held by the editors, Graeme MacRae and Anton Lucas.
Copyright of the individual works is held by their respective author/s.

All rights reserved. Apart from any uses permitted by Australia's *Copyright Act 1968*, no part of this book may be reproduced by any process without prior written permission from the copyright owners. Enquiries should be directed to the publisher.

ISBN: 9781922633590 (paperback)
ISBN: 9781922633606 (pdf)
ISBN: 9781922633613 (epub)

A catalogue record for this book is available from the National Library of Australia

Design by Les Thomas
Typesetting by Jo Mullins
Front cover photograph of John Darling in a forested gorge in Bali: photographer unknown
Back cover photograph of John Darling at his *pondok* Taman Sari, c.1977: Made Wijaya
Poetry translations by Isna Marifa

Printed in Australia by Griffin Press

Contents

Introduction ix
    Graeme MacRae

Part I   In John's Own Words: *Lempad of Bali*

A Note on *Lempad of Bali* 3
    Sara Darling

Foreword to *Lempad of Bali* 5
    Chris Hill

Lempad of Bali: A Memoir of a Master Artist
and the Making of a Film 10
    John Darling

Part II   Behind the Lens: The Filmmaker and His Films

Introduction 41
    Graeme MacRae

Encountering Bali, and Other Indonesian Societies,
through Filmmaking 50
    David Hanan

Lempad of Bali and the Translation of Aesthetics
across Cultures 81
    E. Douglas Lewis

Making *The Healing of Bali* 99
    Sara Darling with Thomas Reuter

Going *Below the Wind* with John Darling 119
    Duncan Graham

Johnny Darling at Murdoch. 126
By Toby Miller

Bleaching Australia 135
Graeme MacRae

Part III   Indonesia: A True Home

John Darling and I Gusti Made Sumung 141
Bruce W. Carpenter

Part IV   John Darling: A Life in Memories

Three Funerals 159
Graeme MacRae

John Darling's Early Life 175
Peronelle Windeyer

John Darling, Old Ubudian 182
Diana Darling

My Favourite Redhead. 186
Made Wijaya

My Friend John Darling 188
Rio Helmi

A Tribute to John 192
Tjokorda Gde Mahatma Putra Kerthyasa

Belonging and Grace 195
James Darling

A Eulogy for John Darling 200
Ace Bourke

A Reflection 210
Peter Gebhardt

Contents

Part V The Artist: Poetry and Paintings

Introduction 217
  Graeme MacRae

Notes from a Ricefield: Poems by John Darling, 1971–77 219

John Darling Filmography 239
Contributors 241

Introduction

Graeme MacRae

This book came out of a series of serendipities. When I first visited Bali briefly in 1977, I was unaware that expats like John Darling were there, in his case already for some years; even he was not yet aware that he was about to become a filmmaker. When I returned to Bali in 1993, this time as a researcher, John was recognised in academic circles as the island's 'most innovative cinematographer'[1] although he was no longer living in Bali He was also well known in both Balinese and expat circles in Ubud. Our paths eventually crossed and our lives became entwined through the neighbourhood (*banjar*) of Taman Klod, where for a short while I filled the space John left as expat-in-residence. But the deeper link was our mutual friend, landlord, teacher and mentor, I Gusti Made Sumung, who was also the son of the famous artist Gusti Nyoman Lempad. It was Gusti Sumung who asked John – at the time a budding poet and Oxford dropout – to make a film of Lempad's cremation, thus igniting John's vocation as a filmmaker.

Gusti Sumung had been dealing with foreign researchers and Baliophiles since the 1930s, and his years with John were in some ways the peak of his long association with them. He lamented the passing of those days and the different sort of foreigners in Bali in later years. But I was the best available at the time, so I briefly filled John's shoes for the last year of Gusti Sumung's life. The three of us met together once only, on one of John's rare visits back to Bali, then again a few months later at Gusti Sumung's (unfilmed) cremation in mid-1994.

After John died in 2011 and I had the privilege of helping his wife Sara sort out his voluminous archives, I came across his journals from his time in Bali. Like mine, they were in local school notebooks bound in batik-patterned paper. I realised on reading them that I was in many ways retracing his footsteps among villages and temples around Ubud, at times quite literally, a couple of decades later. This, I think, is what Gusti Sumung recognised in me, as did other friends in the village of Taman Klod, and our identities became somewhat blended in local thinking. Once, when I arrived in Taman after an absence of several years, a teenager approached me and asked, in somewhat awed tones, 'Are you John Darling?' Balinese now are all too familiar with foreigners, but they still remember those who do more than come and go, and John had already taken on a semi-legendary status in Taman.

The last time I met John was at his home in Perth in mid 2011. I was en route home from Bali, where I had become keenly aware of the aging and passing of his generation of expatriates of the 1970s and 1980s. John had been a key member of this scene which I knew only through the fragmentary reminiscences of some of its veterans. Since then, Bali had been transformed beyond recognition, from 'a user-friendly magic kingdom to a high-density Paradise theme park'.[2] I felt this period had been not only something of a golden age of foreign-Balinese relationships, but a model of a more cosmopolitan

Introduction

kind of development in Bali that might have been. I had in mind a book combining some of these personal reminiscences and stories with more scholarly analysis of the significance of this period. This combination reflects the reality of the time, in which the expats' deep knowledge of Bali took the form not of academic analysis, but of the amateur's fascination with and love of the place – amateur in the original sense of the word as learning 'for the love of it, as a way of life [through] day to day knowing [and] the urge to wander along with that which captures their attention.'[3] That some of these amateurs (such as Michel Picard) later became professional academics is evidence of the depth of their knowledge, but John was the prime exemplar of this combination of the academic and the amateur, and for his entire life he sat (not always easily) astride a line between academia and art.

John agreed with my assessment of that period and was interested in the idea of recording it, and he immediately began searching his vast archives of photographs and film. He also realised that there was another potential film here. We planned to meet again, but a few weeks later his cancer was diagnosed and only now is this book, among other things, a first step toward fruition of that project.

As I hope will become apparent in the pages ahead, John was a complex and interesting person with many endearing qualities, but this alone is hardly enough to justify a book, at least outside the 'vanity press' market. He is best known for his films, all of which were well received and highly regarded by experts and non-experts alike. I have yet to hear him described as a major figure in modern cinema, however. The Bali expatriate scene of the 1970s and 1980s is a field awaiting historical documentation and academic analysis, and John was a key figure in it – enough for another journal article. Finally, he was an early practitioner of what is now known as 'soft' or 'cultural' diplomacy – the use of cultural forms such as the arts to inform, educate and influence awareness and attitudes within and between countries – in this case, the often difficult relationship between Australia and Indonesia, the two countries he knew and loved. It is the combination of these three aspects of John's life and work that I think make him a significant figure, and make this book worth writing (and, we hope, reading). In other words, John was the consummate amateur, the amateurs' amateur. And 'the life's work of the amateur can only be told as story, as biography. It is a story that loops, deviates, circles around, weaving in and out between landmark events.'[4] Hence the form and style of this book.

A year after John died, Sara began the herculean task of sorting out John's voluminous and idiosyncratically organised archives. I asked her whether anyone was planning to write anything about John and was surprised to learn that there were no plans. It was then that I realised that, as with the expatriate stories, it was up to me, and when I raised the idea, Sara agreed – I think because she knew me and I knew John. I offered to help with the sorting, knowing that I would need to go through his papers anyway.

What followed was several years of intermittent research, conversations and requests for contributions, all fitted between other things. What emerged was an eclectic collection of personal anecdotes and reminiscences, reflections, analyses of films and academic essays – fittingly reflecting the multiple facets of the man but presenting challenges of organisation. Then a key piece of John's own writing – about the film that changed his life – which had never been properly published in his lifetime, became available. Our book begins with John's own book and then moves through analyses of his film oeuvre and finally to the man himself.

Introduction

John's account of the subject and making of his first film, *Lempad of Bali*, was first envisaged as a book about Lempad, but between John's health problems and the politics of publishing, this never eventuated. What did eventuate instead was a large multi-authored book, which included a shorter, edited version of John's essay.[5] The essay in its entirety was also published online, but since this is no longer available, we decided to reproduce it here. It places Lempad's story in historical context, but it also contains John's own versions of some of the much-repeated and semi-mythologised episodes of his life, as well as some of his poetry at the time, which provides insight into the romantic sensibility behind his vision of the film.

John was best known as filmmaker, and while his films were widely screened on television in Australia (and later elsewhere), reviewed (mostly favourably) in the media and are well known among Indonesia specialists, I was amazed to find them almost invisible in the academic literature on film. I suspect this reflects their resistance to easy categorisation: are they 'Australian' or 'Indonesian', 'ethnographic', 'documentary' or 'art' films, 'popular' or 'academic' ones? I think the answer is all of the above, because while they sit between these genres, they also span across them. In Part II, we begin this work of discussion and analysis of John's films.

Part II begins with a brief summary of John's career in film. Then David Hanan, formerly of the Department of Visual Arts at Monash University and a specialist on Southeast Asian cinema, has contributed the first detailed academic assessment of John's films, written especially for this book. E. Douglas Lewis, a prominent anthropologist of Indonesia, co-director of a well-known ethnographic film[6] and editor of a book on ethnographic film,[7] has contributed a long essay inspired by reflections on John's first and best-known film *Lempad of Bali*.

He wrote the essay after re-viewing the film nearly forty years on, having had discussions with Rio Helmi and Graeme MacRae.

John's final film *The Healing of Bali* was, according to David Hanan, his most important, alongside *Lempad*. David discusses it in his chapter, but here Graeme MacRae introduces it briefly, ahead of Sara Darling's telling (with help from Thomas Reuter) the story of the making of this film. Closing Part II, Toby Miller, a media studies scholar who worked briefly with John at Murdoch University, has contributed a short chapter returning to the genre of combining scholarly insight (about John's place both in film and in Indonesian Studies) with heartfelt thoughts about a valued friend and mentor.

Together, these essays, including Duncan Graham's review of *Below the Wind*, form the core of the first serious analysis of the filmmaker and his films. But the task is far from complete. Other innovative films such as *Bali Hash* await further analysis, as does John's place in the wider picture of Australian and Indonesian film.

Part III returns to the expat scene of the 1970s and 1980s with Bruce Carpenter's personal reflection on John's (and his own) relationship with his mentor I Gusti Made Sumung. In the process he provides a glimpse of expatriate life in Bali in those days – another project to be researched and written!

Finally we move to John himself – the man behind the films. We begin with Graeme MacRae's weaving-together of the diverse strands of John's life and career in terms of three main stages (A Life in Three Parts) – by no means a complete biography, but perhaps an outline of one. This is followed by an account by Peronelle Windeyer, who knew John's family well during his childhood, of the rarefied world of Geelong Grammar School, where his father was the celebrated headmaster for many years and where John's formative years were spent.

Introduction

John had a great talent for friendship, and when it was clear that he was dying, many old friends reconnected for the last time. And because his life was split between the present in Perth, the past in Bali and a deeper family past in Melbourne, there were three funerals, one in each of these places. Many of his friends and family spoke eloquently at these funerals, and others had written short pieces in various media. We invited some of them to expand these into longer articles, but to our surprise most said they did not feel qualified to say any more about a friend they felt they knew only a part of. Nevertheless, edited versions of some of these elegant, witty and moving tributes form the final part of this book. Diana Darling, Rio Helmi, Made Wijaya, Ace Bourke, James Darling, Peter Gebhardt and Tjokorda Gde Mahatma Putra Kerthyasa speak about John in a way no biographer could do.

The book's final part includes a list of John's work and a selection of his poems, paintings and photography.

For the usual reasons, this book has taken longer to produce than it should have. That it has finally come to fruition is thanks to the generosity and dedication of a number of people. From start to finish, Sara Darling has made it possible and kept nudging me toward completion. Her vast archive of materials from John's own collection have helped me understand the wide-ranging contributions to the art, society and culture of Bali that John has made. At the beginning, the encouragement of Charles Coppell and Jemma Purdey gave us the faith that we had a publisher through the Herb Feith Foundation, and at the end when it had been reborn as the Monash Herb Feith Indonesian Engagement Centre, its new director, Sharyn Graham-Davies also encouraged us and provided critical material support. Greg Bain of Monash Publishing likewise was enthusiastic about publishing when we finally got there and Joanne Mullins and Julia

Carlomagno completed the job. The book is published concurrently in Indonesian thanks to masterly and sensitive translations by Arif Bagus Prasetyo and Imarifa (Isna) Marifa, with invaluable support from Keith Foulcher. These translations as well as editing assistance were made possible by a generous grant from the Nicholas Tarling Charitable Trust and supplementary support from Anton Lucas, Sara Darling and Liza Sutherland.

The final push to completion was spearheaded by Anton Lucas, who brought fresh eyes, editorial skills and commitment. Anton and John had been friends at school, and both came to Indonesia to do fieldwork at the same time. The contributors speak for themselves through their writing, and I am grateful for their patience long after they had probably stopped believing my promises. Many of them also assisted in ways far beyond their written words. Diana Darling, Rio Helmi, Thomas Reuter, the late Made Wijaya (1953–2016) are names that especially spring to mind. Diana also performed a final layer of meta-editing as well as adding valuable insights of her own. Others who did not write did speak, and their words are here between the lines – including John's sisters Jane Gray, Caroline Shearer and Liza Sutherland and her husband Ivan; Ian van Wieringen; David Stuart-Fox; Cody Shwaiko; Jero Asri Kerthyasa; and Andrew Pike of Ronin Films. My thanks to all of them and also (with apologies) to any I have forgotten. My apologies also (as Balinese always say at moments of conclusion) for any mistakes, omissions or excesses for which I am solely responsible. And thanks to my wife, Joan Donaldson, for enduring this most drawn-out of my academic/literary preoccupations.

I conclude with some reflections on the book that has finally emerged. First is that it is not a biography in the sense of a deep exploration of

John's heart and mind – it is more a reflection of his heart and mind in his work and in the eyes of his friends and others. Second is that in all these reflections there are repeated patterns – both of John's character and in the now semi-mythologised stories that people repeat about key moments in his life. These repetitions presented serious challenges of editing, but in some cases they were impossible to avoid entirely. Third, he was a man in whose life women played a large part, beginning with his mother and sisters, climaxing briefly in his marriage to Diana, and ending with the long years with Sara in the latter part of his life. This aspect of his life is perhaps another book, and I have not dwelt upon it here, but there were (always) other girlfriends and lovers in between. You know who you are and how important you were.

But finally, largely (and ironically) absent from the book are John's many Balinese and Indonesian friends, with the exceptions of Rio Helmi and Tjok Gede Mahatma Putra Kerthyasa. John's network of connections across Indonesia was vast and he had many real friends at all levels of society, including the son of one of his village friends whose university studies were paid for by John and Sara. Some of these friends spoke to me of their affection and respect for John, but none of them are writers by inclination, few would have been promising candidates for formal interviews, and many of the most significant ones have since died.[8] This absence is a cause for some unease and regret, but in another way I trust that we hear their voices indirectly through John's films.

Notes

1. Clifford Geertz, 'Foreword' in J. Stephen Lansing, *The Three Worlds of Bali*, New York: Praeger, 1983.
2. Scott Roberts, 'Introduction', in Made Wijaya, *Stranger in Paradise: The Diary of an Expatriate in Bali 1979–80*, Denpasar: Wijaya Words, 1995.
3. Tim Ingold, 'In Praise of Amateurs', *Ethnos* 86, no. 1 (2021), 153–172.
4. Ibid., 161.
5. Bruce Carpenter, John Darling, Hedi Hinzler, Kaja McGowan, Adrian Vickers, Soemantri Widagdo, *Lempad of Bali: The Illuminating Line*, Singapore: Editions Didier Millet, 2014.
6. E.D. Lewis, Timothy Asch, Patsy Asch, *A Celebration of Origins*, Watertown: Documentary Educational Resources, 1993.
7. E.D. Lewis, ed., *Timothy Asch and Ethnographic Film*, London: Routledge, 2004.
8. Among his closest friends in the Balinese community – besides I Gusti Made Sumung – were the stone sculptor I Wayan Cemul, the priest-healer known as Gusti Pekak Balian, the priest Mangku Gede Padang Kerta, the scholar I Gusti Ketut Sangka, the farmer I Gusti Putu Purna (see image no. 16), the painter I Ketut Budiana, and his helper, production assistant and friend I Gusti Nyoman Rupa. All but the last two are deceased. (Diana Darling, pers. com, 20 Nov 2021.)

Part I

In John's Own Words:
Lempad of Bali

A Note on *Lempad of Bali*

Sara Darling

John Austin Campbell Darling (1946–2011)
Filmmaker, poet, academic.

John Darling, my husband, directed (with Lorne Blair) and produced a documentary called *Lempad of Bali* in 1980. This award-winning film was screened on ABC TV and internationally. It tells the life of the 116-year-old Master Artist I Gusti Nyoman Lempad.

The film juxtaposed the wide body of work that Lempad produced over some 100 years including drawings, paintings, sculpture and architecture against Bali's changing history. To locate the relevant archival footage and photos, John travelled to museums in Amsterdam and New York.

Combining this research and the experience surrounding the making of this film, John wrote a short book on Lempad. Chris Hill, a good friend of John, collects Balinese Art and has published in this area. John was delighted that Chris agreed to see this memoir through to completion, and that it was to be available at a major exhibition of Lempad's art at Puri Lukisan Museum in Ubud, Bali in 2014. Sadly, John died before the project was completed.

Duncan Graham wrote John's obituary, which was published in *The Jakarta Post* in January 2012. He stated, 'John was a peaceful man who promoted harmony. He related to everyone, from priests to farmers. His films have helped make Indonesia accessible to the world, particularly Australians.'

Many thanks to Chris Hill (1944–2014), who worked tirelessly to enable John's vision to be realised through sensitively drawing out stories of his life during his final weeks. Chris also provided a depth of knowledge and enthusiasm as he gently re-ordered ancient typed and handwritten documents, along with selecting photographs from John's extensive archive. Chris passed away while visiting the United Kingdom with his wife, Mary. Chris was a kind, generous and wise man. This memoir only reached fruition because of his steady guidance over four years. I am eternally grateful.

Thanks also to Pak Soemantri Widagdo for facilitating the use of Lempad's works in this memoir. In addition, he amended and revised all the Balinese cultural and historical facts in the text.

Finally, thanks to you John for being an amazing dreamer and wonderful storyteller, which you expressed through your films, poetry, art, and love of life, and to those fortunate enough to accompany you on your unique journey.

Foreword to *Lempad of Bali*

Chris Hill

Although he was later to feel more at home in Asia than Australia, John Darling's early life could be described as Melbourne establishment. Born in 1946, he was a student at Geelong Grammar where his father, James R. Darling (later knighted for his services to education and broadcasting) was headmaster. He graduated with honours from the Australian National University and went on to gain a place at Oriel College Oxford, where his father had been a student. His thesis at Oxford was to be on the 'Concept of Empire', but after a year and a half's study he took time out for travel and adventure and set off for Asia. He flew to Kuala Lumpur, where he was instantly seduced by the sights and smells of Southeast Asia. It was his first visit to Asia but everything seemed familiar and he felt as if he belonged there. Oxford and the concept of empire now seemed very distant.

With little money he travelled by train to Singapore, then took a boat to Jakarta, his arrival marking the start of what would be a long relationship with Indonesia. He travelled by train to Yogyakarta and then on to Surabaya, and eventually took a bus and the ferry to Bali. He stayed first in Denpasar, moved to Kuta and then discovered Ubud in central Bali. At that time Ubud was a quiet town with few foreigners; however it was home to many fine Balinese artists and musicians, and increasingly it was becoming a destination for Western artists.

After a few months in Ubud he made his way back to Australia where he travelled and struggled to work out what he wanted to do with his life. Out of respect for his parents' wishes he returned to Britain to resume his studies. Oxford was intellectually stimulating but in spite of coming under the influence of some of the 20th century's great thinkers (he mentioned in particular Isaiah Berlin and Karl Popper) he never finished his degree and headed back to Bali in 1969.

This time Bali well and truly wove its spell on him and the island became his home off and on for nearly 20 years. He later wrote of his early impressions:

> When I first arrived in Bali in the early seventies I was seeking a place in which to develop my obscure talents. Bali provided a perfect environment for such a period of personal development. Not only was it scenically beautiful but also the Balinese themselves had achieved a way of life in harmony with an environment which they have, over centuries, carefully carved and moulded from the rugged terrain of their blessed island. It struck me as a place where it was normal to follow creative pursuits.

John was always a deep thinker and at heart an artist, and this was the early 70s, the height of the hippy era. It is no wonder that he was attracted to the spirituality and aesthetics of the Balinese and that he embraced aspects of Balinese Hinduism. He made many Balinese friends and was also part of a milieu of foreign artists, photographers and anthropologists. Through his friendship with Rudolf Bonnet, who over many years had done much to assist and encourage Balinese artists, he met painters and carvers who were to make a huge contribution to the cultural life of Ubud and surrounding villages. However his meeting with the great artist I Gusti Nyoman Lempad, described by John in the early part of this book, was quite by chance.

He had little money in those early years and claimed that his only possession was an albino cow that lived in his garden; because of its lack of colour it had been shunned by the locals. Living in Bali then was cheap; he said that at the time you could live well but simply on $700 a year.

John is best known as a filmmaker but his early ambition was to be a poet. Writing in the 80s, he describes here how he started to embrace the idea of filmmaking as the means of expressing his feelings for Bali:

> I hope that one day the poetry that I wrote during my first years in Bali will find some recognition. But what happened to me, hardly surprising given the nature of the island, was that Bali subverted me. The way of life around me soon dominated my thinking. It became apparent that here was a story to tell and that I owed it to my friends and neighbours on the island to help them tell it. Furthermore, it became obvious that the medium of film was the means in which to tell these stories. Poetry and film, after all have much in common – imagery, symbols, myth, rhythm and other resonances beyond the immediate.

He started earning money working with visiting filmmakers. He was useful because he knew the language, he had contacts and he was familiar with local customs. He said that he gained the reputation as a 'Mr Fix-It' and would assist with a variety of tasks relating to putting a film together.

When Lempad died in 1978 at an incredible age, estimated at 116 years, his son Gusti Made Sumung suggested that John make a film about the cremation. As well as having a natural understanding of the filmmaking process, John had by now learned from his experience with other filmmakers and he felt ready to embark on his first film. Fortuitously, friend and filmmaker Lorne Blair happened to turn up at just the right time with equipment and film stock and the project was possible. The film became about more than Lempad's cremation, as the artist's long life was shown against a background of episodes from Balinese history. The film was a success and John felt he had found his vocation. From that time on, he directed, produced and researched nine documentary films about Indonesia that have been screened in Australia and internationally. They include the three-part *Bali Triptych* series on Balinese culture, *Bali Hash* and *Below the Wind* and, after the 2002 Bali bombings, he directed and co-produced *The Healing of Bali* with his wife Sara.

John describes in this memoir the making of *Lempad of Bali* and he touches briefly on the research that was needed to find additional imagery and factual information. But what he leaves out is the non-creative side of filmmaking, the administrative work that follows the shooting and editing and in particular the time-consuming and frustrating business of raising funds. Among John's papers I was astonished by the number of files relating to this side of his work. As well as technical skill and creativity, the documentary filmmaker clearly needs perseverance and tenacity to survive the paperwork.

In 2006 *Lempad of Bali* was re-digitalised and made available on DVD with versions in Indonesian and English. It was launched at the Ubud Readers and Writers Festival and the Indonesian version was screened on the soccer ground in Ubud and viewed by over 600 people. It was then shown in Lempad's village, where John had also lived, and it played continuously to family and friends until 2am! Many old friends and family members were recognised by the audience and they regarded the film as a great tribute to Lempad.

As John intended, the text that follows is interspersed with poetry from his Bali years. He was an accomplished poet and his poetry appeared in various publications. In the draft of this memoir that John left, he included a few of his poems. I have added others and interspersed them with his text where they seemed appropriate.

Lempad was a great Balinese artist, perhaps the greatest, but surprisingly little has been written about him, although a major work by Kaja McGowan was published in 2014 to coincide with an exhibition of Lempad's work at Ubud's Museum Puri Lukisan.[1] John always thought that this memoir from someone who knew him and his family well could be of some value, and he was working on it during his final illness. Working with John in the months before he died and then, with Sara's input and encouragement and with help and advice from my wife Mary, seeing the project through to completion has been personally satisfying and a great pleasure. I think John would have been happy with the result.

Note

1   Bruce Carpenter *et al.*, *Lempad of Bali: The Illuminating Line* (Ubud, Museum Puri Lukisan, 2016).

Lempad of Bali

A Memoir of a Master Artist and the Making of a Film

John Darling

Introduction

the old	yang renta
why do they pass away?	mengapa berpulang?
they seem so permanent,	mereka tampak abadi
like wisdom.	seperti wibisana.

The old are revered in Bali. Old men are thought to be wise, women, particularly if they are widows, to be witches. Old age is a rarity in this surprisingly harsh tropical climate where disease has long been rife. As a result the old have an aura of wisdom, carrying with them the memories of times past. I Gusti Nyoman Lempad died in 1978 at the remarkable age of 116 years. He was a young married man in 1883 when the skies were blackened for months by the eruption of Krakatoa. He remembered the age of the independent rajas of Bali before the brutal conquest by the Dutch in 1906 and 1908. In those far off days of the 19th century, Bali was feudal and chivalrous. If somebody was killed in a battle fought with kris and spears, the fighting was halted and would resume only after the necessary immediate death rites had taken place. There was much palace intrigue. The rajas had as many as 50 wives, all eager for the advancement of their sons. Often discreet poisoning took place. At the death of a raja, devoted wives would throw themselves on the funeral pyre.

I first met Lempad in 1970 and knew him for the last eight years of his long life. It was in the early glow that heralds the dawn before the sun rises. I was out walking in the rice-fields looking for a suitable place to enjoy the view of the sun rising beside the great mountain, Agung, which so dominates the small island. An old man with a walking stick approached me along the narrow rice-field path.

minding myself,	sibuk sendiri,
engrossed by the intricacy	terserap dalam seluk-beluk
of a seedling's growth:	tumbuhnya tunas:
startled!	terkejut!
by an old man's friendly call.	bapak tua memanggilku, ramah.

He could tell that I was trying to find an unimpeded view of the mountains. He beckoned me to follow him and so the glory of the morning was laid out before us. We sat on the grass of a padi bank to appreciate the short moment of beauty that begins the day.

half-waning moon	bulan separuh pudar
at dawning day;	saat fajar menyingsing;
on a lotus cloud	di atas awan teratai
the stupa mountain rests.	terbujur gunung stupa.
through a dew-jewelled web	dari sela sarang laba-laba beruntai
I glimpse the lavender	embun
mountain:	kutengok gunung lembayung:
the ascending sun melts the dew	mentari melangit, melebur embun
and the great mountain drifts	dan gunung nan luhur redup
away.	perlahan.

Conversation was almost impossible between us as I was only new to Indonesia. Even if I had been able to speak Indonesian it would have been little use; as I was to discover when I came to know him better, he only spoke Balinese. At the time I did not realise that he was out in the field to check his rice crop.

A few days later Lempad's son, I Gusti Made Sumung, came up to me in the street in Ubud and said that they had a small house available and that his father would like me to stay with them. Through the generosity of his son, I was welcomed into this large family and spent many of the next twenty years as their guest in Bali. I built a house on Lempad land close to where I first met this remarkable and spiritual old man.

Black rope and bamboo make my house,	Tambang hitam dan bambu membentuk rumahku,
I have a mouse in my straw roof	Celurut tinggal di atap jeramiku
Frogs make comforting music through the night.	Semalaman katak lantunkan musik mendayu.
My lamp casts shadows on the plants	Tanaman berbayang dari sinar pelitaku
Dim in my distance a cat stalks quietly by:	Redup di kejauhan seekor kucing menyeluduk tanpa suara:
I can see a few stars	Aku bisa lihat beberapa bintang
But they are of another world.	Tapi mereka dari alam berbeda.

On 25 April 1978, in the village of Taman in the fertile hills of central Bali, the island's greatest artist of the century died at the conservatively estimated age of 116 years. I Gusti Nyoman Lempad's age was cause enough for wonderment but the magnificent body of fine art that he

left behind is a much greater tribute to this unusual man. He lived his creative and fulfilling life though the most traumatic century of Balinese history. Through these difficult times, his way of life and his creative work enriched the already rich culture of Bali. His spiritual development and his faith in the values of Balinese religion was a constant source of encouragement to his community through the rapid changes that dominated the 20th century.

Lempad claimed that the reason for his longevity was that, as a young man, an old, respected sage had suggested to him that if he maintained a simple life, kept clear of politics and observed his sometimes demanding responsibilities to the community, he would live a long and fulfilled life. Although the Balinese have long known the secrets of reading and writing, Lempad never learnt these skills and depended on inspiration from the vital theatrical traditions of Bali, though he learnt to draw the characters that made his own name in both Balinese and Latin script. Now that he is dead, the Balinese people themselves are amazed at his vision and breadth of abilities. They wonder if their small island will ever produce another like him.

The Long Life of I Gusti Nyoman Lempad

An Auspicious Arrival

Lempad was born, the third of four brothers who all passed away well before him, in Bedulu, close to Pakrisan, the most sacred river on the island, which flows through the heartland of ancient Balinese culture. On its banks stand some of the most splendid remains of the ancient kingdoms. In his youth, Lempad frequently bathed in the springs of a tenth century Buddhist monastery hewn from solid rock.

Throughout his creative life, Lempad was to recall in his sculpture and architecture the weathered images of these shrines. The family rice-fields faced onto one of the most extraordinary works of art on the island. Experts are unable to date or classify these carvings, though they believe them to be the creation of one man.

Folklore claims that the beautiful carvings on the rock wall at Yeh Pulu are the work of the mythological giant Kebo Iwa who carved them with his thumbnail. There is a personal vision in this particular sculpture outside traditional form, which it appears influenced the young Lempad.

The Gianyar district, of which Bedulu is part, has witnessed two periods of historical interest. The first was in mythological times, the second began in the unsettled times of the 1840s when the Dutch first began their attempts to subdue and control the island. The first Raja of Gianyar emerged as the ruler of a new and distinct state in the late 18th century.

Previously, the territory now called Gianyar had been divided among the kingdoms of Klungkung, Bangli, Mengwi and Badung. By the 1800s the Dewa Agung, the ruler of Klungkung and the lineal descendent of the Majapahit kingdom, had lost much of his political power and prestige after being defeated by his eastern neighbour, Karangasem. The vacuum in power was exploited by an ambitious village leader of noble descent who by means of deceit, poisonings and war, gained mastery over his neighbouring villages and then expanded his control over the vast area.

This upstart was not welcomed by the other established rulers of Bali and throughout the 19th century there was a confused series of wars between the kingdoms of southern Bali. Finally, hard-pressed on all sides, the ruler of Gianyar formed an agreement with the

Dutch government which was formalised in 1900. While the Dutch struggled to subdue the rest of Bali, which climaxed in the horrors of the 1906 and 1908 *puputan*, Gianyar flourished under this protectorate arrangement. The palace of Gianyar and the lesser royal courts of the kingdom became the centres of a renaissance of traditional Balinese art forms.

Lempad was born into this period of intrigue and petty wars around 1862. His father, I Gusti Ketut Mayukan, was also a fine craftsman, being particularly renowned for his abilities in making masks for the *topeng* (mask dance drama). When he was still a young boy of ten years or so he was assisting his talented father to create a magic *barong* cult-mask for the people of the village of Pedjeng, near Bedulu, when his father was summoned by the ruler of the district whose palace was at Blahbatu. Lempad's father, fearing this summons, asked a friend in the palace what it was about. The friend warned him that due to misinformation passed on by a jealous rival he was about to be exiled to the dry and barren island of Nusa Penida southeast of Bali.

Lempad's son, I Gusti Made Sumung, described this event:

> My grandfather was getting too successful for some people's liking. His star was on the ascendant and this was causing jealousy. So he asked the Prince for permission to move away. But a good friend heard that the Prince was planning to exile him and his entire family to a remote island. That night Lempad and his family slipped out of Bedulu and eventually came to Ubud, which at that time was a minor Princedom that could not even boast a royal palace.

The ambitious Prince of Ubud was quick to take advantage of young Lempad's talents. He was apprenticed to a leading priestly caste of craftsman of the district and from this man he learnt most of his skills. A palace to rival those of the great kingdoms was built with his help. Living in the palace Lempad was quick to learn the many skills required in building. In the evenings he would listen to readings from the great classics and thus he developed his philosophy of life. As the prestige of the region spread, temples and palaces sprouted above the mud walls and Lempad was kept constantly busy, and the Ubud of today is largely of his making. Lempad's artistic style in the formative years was firmly set within the traditional mould of Balinese design. But the quirkish humour that was to dominate his later work was already in evidence.

Undagi Lempad, the Complete Artist

During his lifetime, Lempad earned the spontaneous honorific title of *undagi*. This title is bestowed by the general feeling of the community as a token of respect to the skills of a master craftsman. An *undagi* is a builder, an architect, a painter, a sculptor, a dancer and a choreographer. Lempad was all of these; he designed and carved temples; he made many of the wonderful and benign beasts of magic called *barong*; for royal cremations he was often called upon to oversee the making of the magnificent paraphernalia that accompanied such illustrious persons on their last journeys; he carved masks out of wood, reliefs and standing sculptures out of stone and drew superbly with a confident and exotic line; and in his own village he was the instigator of a marvellous dance group. However, due to his humility Lempad never claimed the title of *undagi* for himself.

Lempad was the epitome of the complete Balinese artist and man. His life of light was a victory against the powers of darkness and underlying all his creative work was the understanding that art is not for the self-gratification of the artist but for the continuing welfare of the community – and hence for the glory of the gods that are the determiners of mankind's existence. He believed that he was re-incarnated on this earth to create what the gods directed. He was happy to make whatever people with a pure heart requested of him, but most important to him were the cremation towers that transport souls of the dead to the other world, and the cremation bulls which make the journey a smooth one. For Lempad, as for all Balinese, his life was no more than one adventure in a continuous cycle of incarnation.

During the late 1880s and 1890s the kingdom of Ubud was engaged in a series of small wars with neighbouring Mengwi and Negari. Ubud was generally successful in these wars. Lempad served his new masters as a warrior and ambassador.

Lempad married, as is Balinese tradition, while still a young man of about twenty years. He remembered that this was before the great eruption of Krakatoa in 1883. He then moved out of the palace into his own house on land sold to him by the *cokorda* (prince) of Ubud. Over the years Lempad's new home took on the air of a small museum, filled with the art he created for his own pleasure. Unfortunately, over the years it became apparent that his wife was unable to have children. So, in about 1910, following Balinese custom he married her younger sister as a second wife. The three of them lived together in harmony bringing up their five children until the first wife's death in the 1940s. Lempad's second wife, his widow and the mother of his children, was a serene old lady who was still making the family's offerings when well over a hundred years old.

Chaos Comes to Bali

There is a tension everywhere	Resah dimana-mana
As the thunder grumbles slowly	Saat geledek lamban bergumam
Nearer	Lebih dekat
The sky darkens	Langit berubah gelap
And the midday stillness	Dan hening tengah hari
Is disturbed by rebel eddies of the wind	Direcoki riak-riak liarnya angin

The 1940s brought the Second World War to Bali. Fulfilling the ancient prophesy of the Javanese sage, Joyoboyo, the yellow monkey came from the east and put the white ox in a cage. The image of Western man's invincibility was demolished. The Japanese promised friendship and liberation, but the Indonesians were soon to discover that one master had simply been replaced by another. Eventually the tides of war changed and the Japanese were expelled, after which followed a four-year war of independence against the returning Dutch.

During these years of chaos, Lempad retreated into a meditative state and produced almost no works of art. Family and friends were convinced that he would soon die. He later explained that the disarray of the world obliged him to turn inwards in search of personal serenity. His only major work of this time is the remarkable carving of his ancestors, which he carved in a hard white stone for his family temple in Bedulu. It is a work of quiet religious power.

New Work Aged Ninety

Elusive knowledge,	Ilmu yang tak mudah diraih,
A product of receptive seeing	Hasil mengamati, menyerap
Coming to us	Datang pada kita
In black and white	Dalam hitam dan putih
And hot and cold	Panas dan dingin
And nature rhythms,	Dan irama alam,
Oh what are we	O apakah kita
But receptacles	Kalau bukan sekedar wadah
Which occasionally overflow	Yang sesekali meluap.

Few believed it possible that at the age of 90, he was to begin a remarkably creative artistic renaissance. When the prince of Ubud was released from imprisonment he wished to give thanks to the gods for bringing an end to troubled times. He commissioned Lempad to design and build a temple to Dewi Saraswati, the goddess of wisdom, knowledge and the arts. This magnificent temple with its beautifully proportioned lotus pond is now a tourist attraction in central Ubud. Inside the temple Lempad himself carved the giant freestanding figure of Jero Gede Mecaling, the demon of the sea, as a guardian for the southern aspect. In the northeast corner he designed and supervised the building and carving of a great padmasana, an altar to the Supreme God-Head. On the back of this altar is the image of the goddess Saraswati riding on her goose. It is appropriate that Lempad's most monumental work should be dedicated to the goddess of wisdom and the arts.

Soon after building this temple he was engaged by the village of Ubud to re-build the great gate for the village Pura Desa (community temple), which is on the main roadway close to the centre of the village. In 1955 he built a new great gateway crowned with the magnificent face of the protector Boma for the important state temple of Pura

Samuan Tiga in Bedulu. Pura Samuan Tiga's annual festival was being held at the time of his death. The evening before he died he sent his daughter here to give offerings. She had no idea that through her he was notifying the gods of his intended passing.

His incredible burst of energy since turning 90 was not confined to monumental architecture and carving, his painting style also underwent a renaissance. His line became even more refined and dramatic as can be seen in the painting of the 'Dreaming of Dharmawangsa' which now hangs in the Puri Lukisan Museum in Ubud. In another painting the great god Siwa decides to test his wife's faithfulness by sending her to earth to get milk from a virgin cow (see image no. 10). Disguising himself as a handsome cow-herd, Siwa offers to provide it for her if she will mate with him. Determined to fulfil her task, she eventually agrees, but, suddenly distressed by her own unfaithfulness, she pulls free and Siwa's sperm falls to the ground. From this grows the demonic and destructive Bhatara Kala. The three-petal symbol on one fang indicates his semi-divine status. The western visitor on the other is Lempad's ironical addition to the legend. Bhatara Kala is the god of catastrophe.

Lempad did not forget his duties to the art community and in the 1950s he became the founder-teacher at Golongan Pelukis art school in Ubud. In 1956 he assisted Rudolf Bonnet with the building of the Puri Lukisan Museum in Ubud. In 1961 he was called upon to design and build the *naga banda* – the cosmic serpent which guides the soul of the deceased to the appropriate heaven – and the *lembuh* (cremation bull) for the cremation of the last Raja of Gianyar. Even in 1976, two years before his death and at the age of 114, he designed a *naga banda* for the cremation of one of the princes of Ubud, and supervised his grandson in its building.

In 1970, on the 25th anniversary of the founding of the Republic of Indonesia, Lempad was the recipient of the first Piagam Anugrah Seni award for his contribution to Indonesian art. This was a due acknowledgment from his own government, which parallels the fact that many of his fine works, including a full *barong*, carved gamelan stands and drawings are held by many museums of the world. In 1976 Lempad presented a drawing of the Balinese legend of the moon eclipse to the American astronaut Ronald E. Evans. His family obtained a television set just two months before his death providing a startling glimpse to Lempad of the world the tourists came from. I have sometimes wondered what this experience meant to the grand old man.

In his final years Lempad had already started to break his links with the material world. For days in a row he would sit in silent meditation or gazing at his works of the past. He spent the last two years of his life on his final unfinished sculpture, a mask of a young soul. He had journeyed through the most traumatic century of Balinese history from the age of omnipotent princes to that of television and astronauts.

The End of a Long Life

> My father had heard during many discussions in the palaces that it was best to die when the sun was rising in the northeast. So he waited during his last year for the proper time to die. Many people asked him why it was taking him so long to die? He replied: I cannot yet see the true path. I must wait until the sun rises in the northeast. Then I can die. (I Gusti Made Sumung, from the film *Lempad of Bali*)

Lempad died a conscious death. He chose an appropriate day on the Balinese calendar for such a transition. 25 April 1978 was the day *kajeng kliwon* of the Balinese calendar; the sun in its cycle was at its northern most point close to the sacred mountain where it is believed the gods and ancestors dwell. Three temples, all of importance to him (Pura Besakih, the state temple; the Pura Dalem the death temple of his village; and Pura Samuan Tiga in Bedulu where he was born and for which he had carved the great gate in 1955), were in the process of having their temple festivals at the time. This is when the Balinese people believe the gods are in attendance in the world of man. Before he died, he called his family to him, asked to be washed and then dressed in white. After blessing his descendants and asking them to complete whatever he had left unfinished, he died at 8:30am under the gentle caresses of his family.

On 25 April 1978, Lempad set out on the hazardous journey across the bridge of death, back to the place where all things originate. A temple-bell tolled his passing. It called the village community to the aid of his family. Together they must prepare the body for the cycle of rituals that will eventually lead to one of the world's most impressive death rites – the Balinese cremation.

Balinese religion is a dynamic blending of Hindu-Buddhism and ancient Indonesian animism. There are clear distinctions between the material body, the soul and a third element, which we might call the astral being. This is composed of several subtle and immaterial elements that form the being. The soul and the astral being are the eternal elements that continue into future incarnations. At death, the return to the realm of ancestors is but a transitional phase – a regeneration – before reincarnation within the same family.

The purification of Lempad's body was supervised by the village priest-healer, a family friend. The corpse was anointed with a sweet-smelling concoction of ground blossoms, rice flour and egg yolk; a powerful symbol of regeneration. Family and friends bathed him with holy water. Although the Balinese know birth and death to be a time when evil forces can threaten the living, they accept it as their duty to personally prepare the body of a loved one. They regard the western habit of assigning this task to a professional as barbaric.

Mirrors in the eyes assure clear vision in the next incarnation, a metal comb on the mouth guarantees strong, sharp teeth, and a ruby ring on the tongue promises eloquent speech. Each of his chakras – the power points that tie his astral being together – was adorned with offerings. Thus dressed, the corpse was held aloft and all female descendants passed underneath – an acknowledgement of the descent and the origin of their fertility.

Once the body was wrapped and laid out to await cremation, attention concentrated on the preparation of the soul for the journey of the astral being and the soul. A lantern was hung at the door of the house so that Lempad's wandering spirit could be guided back to his material body, lying at rest in the main pavilion of the house. A high priest of the most elevated caste, through secret formulas of hand gestures, voice and heart, prepares Holy Water. Family and friends then pray and extend their blessings to the soul of the deceased. The Balinese do not grieve unnecessarily over the death. For them, this life is no more than one adventure in a continuous cycle of incarnation.

Cremations play their part in preserving the arts because everyone in the community is able to contribute according to their talents. Soon after Lempad's death, preparations began on his cremation bull and tower. Craftsmen from throughout the district, who had been students of Lempad, contributed their multiple talents. Almost the entire village community turned out every day to assist in the work. The tower had seven roofs indicating his caste; a prince would have nine and a king, as a descendent of Majapahit, eleven. The bull's head, spine and legs were carved from wood. The stomach was made from a bamboo basket in which the corpse was to be placed for the burning. On the street outside the house, Lempad's grandson I Gusti Nyoman Sudara, who has inherited some of his grandfather's talent, worked on carving the bull. The Lempad house stands on the busy main street of Ubud, now renowned for its artists and as a major tourist destination.

Over a period of twenty days, raw blocks of wood were transformed into striking masks of supernatural beings to adorn the tower, which would carry Lempad's body to the place of cremation. One would become Boma, a powerful guardian figure seen on all temple gateways in Bali. Another, a Garuda, the mythological great eagle, would assist with the flight of the soul to the heavens. All art in Bali is transient, even the soft volcanic sandstone wears away with time, but the towers and bulls for cremations are the most startling example of this. The tower and bull are the results of weeks of inspired artistry; they are transformed to ashes in the span of a few hours.

These lavish preparations were costly but the family's finances in this case were not overly strained. All labour was provided free and many of the materials contributed by friends. The black velvet for the bull, for example, was a gift from the prince of Ubud. The family's main expense was food as a feast was provided for the voluntary helpers every day. Pork is the principal meat for such feasts. The pork is minced before being mixed with coconut gratings, lemon and herbs, then pasted onto a bamboo skewer before being grilled to become a delicious variety of satay.

Traditionally men do most of the cooking for communal feasts, as the women are kept constantly busy preparing the essential offerings. Lempad's surviving second wife supervised the making of this multitude of offerings that were required for the cremation rite. Rice pastry was kneaded into complex forms before being fried in coconut oil. Despite their transient nature, offerings are among the most refined art forms of the island. An important offering effigy at the cremation is the *angenan* as it represents the deceased's spiritual being. A rice-filled coconut shell represents the heart, twined threads the mind and an eggshell lamp the soul. It is placed in the bull to be burned with the body.

At Pura Samuan Tiga, where in 1955 Lempad had carved a great Boma head, Lempad's son, I Gusti Made Sumung, had a white cloth inscribed by the local priest. The priest drew symbols of the various elements that make up Lempad's astral being – the *kanda empat* (the four spiritual brethren) and the chakra points. The Balinese believe that without such a cloth the spiritual being would break up, get lost, and never reach its proper place. The shroud (*kajang*) is placed on the body of the deceased and accompanies it to cremation.

Every night until cremation, the immediate family kept constant vigil. They were assisted on some nights by traditional entertainment. The shadow puppet play is one of Bali's most important dramatic forms in which ancient legends are told by a single puppeteer. Through these performances the audience can glimpse the world of their ancestors; a monochrome image of a richly-coloured reality beyond. Puppet plays were a great influence on Lempad's drawing. Through a series of storybooks he had used the legends of Bali to express the philosophy of the island. In one of the stories he illustrated that when a young man's bride died unexpectedly, he tore his hair and clutched her dead body to him. The great god Siwa visited earth and pointed out that the body is but a cast-off shell. While the husband clung to an illusion, she in fact lived on in another world. Admitting his folly, the husband decided to search for her in the realm of the ancestors. As Lempad told it, the journey was a quest for self-knowledge. It appeared that Lempad had been preparing for his last journey for some time.

Cremation

On the night before the actual day of Lempad's cremation a series of important rituals took place. The high priest prepared a special holy water, both for the last prayers of family and friends and for the final consecration of the material body and soul of the much-loved master artist. A priest puppeteer assisted the high priest in this ritual by performing without a screen (*wayang lemah*). Just a thread of cotton tied between two branches of the ever-sprouting dadap tree divided the audience from the realm of ancestors.

Gusti Biang, Lempad's daughter and eldest child, wafted incense and prayer over the body. Family and friends then prayed together before receiving holy water.

A platform piled high with offerings symbolising the material world was then placed in the centre of the family compound. Animals, plants, farming instruments, wayang puppets and carving tools were amongst those objects represented. A pole that has been blessed by the priest represented the astral being – the four spiritual brethren and chakra points. This pole was attached by a symbolic red umbilical cord to an offering, which was carried like a young baby and represented the soul. This procession circled the platform, which represented the material world, three times. Then with loud cries this symbol of the material world was thrown into the air and destroyed. This symbolically severed the soul and astral being from any last attachments to the material world. Now the task of destroying Lempad's body by fire could commence the next day.

Early the next morning the tower, a symbol of the three worlds – earth, mankind and the heavens, which reflects the holy mountain of Gunung Agung – was placed out on the street with the black bull. The sole physical purpose of the tower is to transport the body of

Lempad one mile to the cremation ground near the death temple. A gamelan orchestra arrived to entertain during the morning hours while the courtyard of the house was filled with guests who had come to pay their last respects. An old man had remembered that the wooden instrument stands had been carved by Lempad many years before, and he had brought the gamelan to give due honour to the deceased.

The streets of Ubud were packed with people, both Balinese and tourists. The hotels on the beaches to the south were informed of a cremation and busloads of tourists, most of them unaware of who was actually being cremated, filled the road between Lempad's house and the cremation ground. One interested guest was Paloma Picasso, a curious and coincidental link between two of the greatest and most prolific artists of the twentieth century.

At around midday, the body of Lempad was carried from the house in a sarcophagus on which sat one of the princes of Ubud, symbolically showing that Lempad had spent much of his life as a servant of the palace. Once the body was placed in the tower and accompanied by a cacophony of gongs, the procession made its way to the place of burning. At the cremation ground in front of the temple of Durga, dedicated to the goddess of death – a temple to which Lempad had, in earlier years, contributed his carvings – the body was transferred from the tower to the bull in preparation for the cremation. The black velvet of the bull was slashed and the body lifted into the bull. The *pedanda* (high priest) placed the angenan, the shroud and other offerings in with the body. The body was doused with holy water to guide Lempad's spirit in the annihilation of the hells attached to earthly life and to point out the path to the seven heavens of his caste.

The bull and the tower were then set alight. All things concerned with death are regarded by the Balinese as ritually unclean and therefore polluting and must be burnt. As the fire consumed the bull, its torso collapsed to reveal the burning corpse suspended on wires. Lempad's wife and friends threw gifts of betel nut into the flames; a last taste of earthly pleasures to accompany him on his long journey.

On the day following the cremation, the final disposal of Lempad's body took place. The few bits of human ash and bone that survived the flames were gathered together. No human remains could be overlooked, as they might lure him back and bind him forever to the material world. Then Lempad's descendants took turns, using their left hands, on which they wore heavy bracelets of old Chinese coins, to grind these remains into a fine ash. Later that night, at a beach 20km away, the ashes of the deceased were cast into the sea. The mortal remains of I Gusti Nyoman Lempad and memories spanning five generations were finally disposed of. The old man could become a young soul and gain rest with his ancestors in the land of origin.

Hear the regular thump of waves on black sand, this breezeless night.	Dengar irama dentum ombak pada pasir hitam, di malam nirbayu ini.
the priest's bell rings echoes from bright stars in ancient ritual: descending generations pray in homage and farewell to the ashes of the material body of an aged and honoured ancestor just gathered from the imperious charr'd bull.	lonceng pedanda berbunyi gema dari bintang cemerlang dalam upacara lawas: turun-temurun berdoa memberi hormat dan pamitan pada abu jasad kasar seorang leluhur tua dan disegani baru saja dikumpulkan dari lembu berwibawa hangus terbakar.

beyond the waves, from a becalmed canoe, these mortal remains are thrown into black sea waters	jauh dari pecahnya ombak, dari sampan terdiam, serpih kehidupan fana dilempar ke dalam perairan laut kelam
a soul rises with the crescent moon this breezeless night.	roh bangkit bersama bulan sabit pada malam nirbayu ini.

For twelve days the family anxiously awaited a sign from their ancestor that something may have been overlooked. If it had been, further complicated rituals would have been required. No sign came and so on the twelfth dawn they descended to the same beach of black volcanic sand to bid a tender and final farewell to the greatest Balinese artist of the century.

Lempad and Western Influence

Classical Balinese Art

To provide some context for Lempad's art, particularly his paintings, it is useful to look at the origins of the tradition that he was to put his distinctive mark upon. Balinese painting owes its origins to the new courts that settled at Gelgel, near Klungkung, in southern Bali. This style of painting, using natural pigment on hand-woven cloth, is derived from the two-dimensional cut-out figures of the wayang kulit – the shadow puppet theatre of Java and Bali. Variously called Wayang or Kamasan, it is still practised today in the village of Kamasan, whose craftsmen are supported by the court of the Dewa Agung, the leading Raja and lineal descendent of the old Hindu-Javanese Majapahit empire.

In ancient times, Balinese artisans were multi-faceted. They could sculpt, draw and paint, although the latter medium was only expressed through three definite forms: *ider-ider* (long scrolls), *tabing* (squares) and *langse* (hangings). Before the 20th century, such paintings were commissioned as decorations for the palace or temple, but because of their religious subject matter and ultimate destinations they remained unsigned. In Bali, the painter was traditionally a craftsman working for the greater glory of his gods, or for the rajahs and princes who represented the gods on earth.

By the end of the 19th century, armed conflicts between rival kingdoms caused the Dutch to become more involved with island affairs. Between 1908 and 1938, Dutch administrators did their best to preserve Balinese culture by interfering as little as possible in the island's centuries-old traditions. But while they brought peace, they also brought taxes and a new wave of tourists. Throughout the 1930s, the number of wealthy globetrotters visiting Bali from Europe and America increased dramatically, drawn by the lure of exotic dance performances and the opportunity to acquire articles of value for next to nothing. The new wave of visitors also brought much-needed cash, thus changing the traditional structure of artistic patronage. It was against this background that one of Bali's greatest artistic renaissances began.

Western Influence and New Creative Possibilities

Among the westerners who arrived on Bali's shores were already-established European artists, including Walter Spies, Rudolf Bonnet and Miguel Covarrubias. They brought with them not only a background in classical and avant-garde western art, but also the necessary tools of their profession: water colours, oil paints, pre-cut paper and canvas.

Within this context of change, new styles of Balinese painting came into being, to a large extent influenced by these artists. The rigid conventions of the traditional style were no longer binding. Instead of illustrating stories from the great Hindu epics, some Balinese artists began to depict scenes of everyday life and nature in their work.

In 1927, Klungkung was still the centre for traditional painting, while new art was springing up in Ubud, Batuan and Sanur. Although both Sanur and Ubud had close contact with the European artists, the theory that Balinese art leaped from 'medieval' to 'modern' because of the intervention of foreigners ignores the distinctly individual achievement of artists who were independently creative before 1930.

The most important of Balinese art's transitional figures was I Gusti Nyoman Lempad. Rudolf Bonnet, the Dutch artist and, after the war the founder of the Puri Lukisan Museum in Ubud, related to me that when he first arrived in Ubud in early 1929, Lempad already appeared to be an old man. Lempad was in his late 60s when Walter Spies, who arrived in Bali in 1927, gave him his first paper. Lempad was at this time assisting Spies build his house at Campuan near Ubud. His earliest known drawing is held by the Tropenmuseum in Amsterdam. It tells the Rajapala story in which the seven celestial nymphs, symbols of divine inspiration, fly down to bathe in an earthly pool where they are spotted by a young prince who, by stealing the scarf of one them, persuades her to remain and give him a child. This earliest drawing on paper is still and unsure, though it already indicates the dexterity that became his trademark. In the 50 years following, the pen and ink drawings that flowed from Lempad's hand were never simply a naive imitation of European techniques. While his style had its origins in tradition, he developed an unusual freedom in exploring the symbolic richness of the legends of his homeland.

Between 1935 and 1940, the new art of Bali was in full bloom under the guidance of the Pita Maha (Noble Aspiration), an artists' organisation founded by the Prince of Ubud, Cokorda Gde Agung Sukawati, with the guidance of Walter Spies and Rudolf Bonnet. Although it appears an unlikely appointment, Lempad, who could neither read nor write was recorded as the secretary of this organisation. By providing new materials and encouragement, but no deliberate tutoring, these men helped launch a renaissance of the arts – fired by the tourists who were actually prepared to pay money for art – much to the amusement of the Balinese.

More than 150 artists from all over Bali joined Pita Maha. This organisation provided both inspiration and a forum of consultation for members, as well as quality control and distribution for their works. This new set of group ties lifted members from the context of normal village life and provided them with a sense of community in the confrontation between their secluded island and the values of the west.

The 1930s were a particularly creative time for Lempad. It was during this decade that he spent some time working with the Dutch sculptor, Van der Norda. The life-size Pied Piper of Hamlyn and the freestanding Balinese couple in ceremonial dress which still dominate the family compound are products of this period. He rebuilt the family ancestor temple in Bedulu, including the remarkable top-heavy gateway of great stone blocks.

It was delightfully described to us by I Gusti Made Sumung:

> When the big earthquakes of 1963 struck, this was the only great gate around that suffered no damage. What makes it different from others, if I may say so, is that it slightly resembles the work of Kebo Iwa, the giant. Just look at that stone! He used it just as it came from the quarry. He didn't chop it up small to then make

it big…(as is usual in Bali)…If you want to make something big why not use a big stone. It is like Gusti Lempad himself, from the outside it looks very simple, but inside, the engineering is very complicated.

During the latter years of the 1930s Lempad gained a reputation amongst the small western community on the island for his erotic drawings and his books of drawings on largely Balinese folk-tales, such as Pan Brayut, Dukuh Siladri, Jayaprana, Gagak Turas and Sutasoma. This, along with the fact that his son I Gusti Made Sumung acted as secretarial assistant to Jane Belo, a long term resident of the island who was married to the famous musicologist and composer Colin McPhee, attracted attention to him. Writing at a later date (I believe the early 1940s) Jane Belo described their impressions of Lempad. He was then 78 years old with another 38 years to live.

> We first met him in 1932 when we came to live at Tjampoean. At that time he looked much as he does now, he had the same mild gentle ways, was always slow to speak and most polite. But he did not seem as feeble as he does now. I remember I was so very much impressed by his good manners, his modesty, kindness and generosity that I said to Walter (Spies) he seemed to me the perfect type of Balinese aristocrat. Walter agreed, and we laughed because the Tjokordas were so different. If they were all like Goesti Njoman, we said, what a different place Oeboed (Ubud) would be. (At this time I considered a Goesti to be pretty highborn, possible because I knew the royal families of Badoeng and Kapal were Goestis, and I did not realize what a step down from a Tjokorda a goesti is considered to be in Oeboed.) He was at the time also much more prosperous than he is now, one felt rather ashamed to ask him to make anything for money, and one had to urge and press it upon him. He wanted to give everything away.

Margaret Mead, writing in 1938, also commented on his refinement of character:

> He is a gentle, worried man, riddled by the fear of debt, and the burden of gratitude. I do not feel that he is anxious, however. Slender, worn down by exertion, with very old-fashioned manners, unwilling ever to make a point in his own favour, incapable of bargaining...The two wives, who are sisters, one childless, are both slender fine grained women ... They live right in Oeboed, with a great courtyard filled with high taro plants, and a permanent *taring* (thatched palm-leaf covering) under which work is done, giving the place the effect of a tumble down winter garden. There are beautiful carved bales (pavilion), carved by his father who also was a great toekang (craftsman).

On his work Mead commented:

> He has a very distinctive style, a line that is always recognizable, and all attempts to use his tjontos (sketches) or imitate him always show up ... But his method of work is exceedingly alien to any western sentimental valuations; he makes a tjonto on tracing paper, with a firm, finished line, and then lets people order from the tjontos. When they have made a selection he sews their batches together and puts the identical design on white paper. His sketching line is lovely. He has always done every type of work, practically; he does leather work, stone work, woodcarving. He says Walter taught him how to work with paper and paint ... He works all the time and very hard. (These quotes from Belo and Mead are from their field-notes in the 'Mead Collection' held by the Library of Congress, Washington D.C.)

The Making of the Film *Lempad of Bali*

A few hours after Lempad's death I called at the family compound to offer my services for the demanding and elaborate tasks that make up the traditional Balinese rituals of death. To these people death is not normally a time of great sadness but merely a transition within the endless cycle of re-incarnation. They believe that the spirit and soul is continually re-incarnated within the same family-descent group. With a man such as Lempad who had unquestionably lived a rewarding life, there was no sadness in evidence. What was important though was that the rituals and accompanying paraphernalia should be correct in every way so as to assure the successful destruction of his material body and his soul's true liberation from the world of man.

By the time I reached the compound, many of the village people were already there. They were delivering coconuts and bamboo and beginning to prepare those things that would be necessary for the ceremonies to follow. I offered to do whatever I could to assist in this great work. Made Sumung, who was fully aware of my incompetence as a craftsman of bamboo and wood, took me aback by suggesting that I should make a film of the cremation. My immediate reply was that this was an impossibility as I had no equipment or even film stock let alone expertise for such a task. However, strange things have been known to happen in this island of the gods. Later that day I ran into a filmmaker friend, Lorne Blair, who had just arrived in Bali from a filming trip in the interior of Kalimantan (Borneo). Lorne still had his equipment and luckily two unused rolls of film. We started filming immediately and were able to record the never-before-filmed ritual of the washing of the body of the deceased.

The second unusual co-incidence of that day was that I received a cable from friends in Australia informing me that they were coming to Bali in a few days and was there anything that I needed. After much difficulty with the antiquated telephone system, I was able to arrange that we should receive enough raw film stock to cover the complete death rituals, as they progressed over the next twenty days and nights. Co-incidences such as these, which continued throughout the making of the film, convinced us that the spirit of Lempad was aiding us in our endeavours. Certainly his presence was very much in evidence during the twenty days that saw the making of the elaborate seven-tiered tower which carried his body to the cremation ground and the magnificent noble bull in which his body was burnt. These two splendid examples of the transient arts of Bali were created by Lempad's descendants and those he had taught during his long, creative life.

The film we made shows the craftsmen at work constructing the tower and bull. It also follows the rituals which part the soul and the astral being from the mortal body and the material world in close detail, including the burning of the body and the throwing of the ashes into the sea. However, while we were filming these activities, it became apparent to us that in making a film about such a man as Lempad, it was not enough to purely record the Balinese ritual of death which, after all are pretty much the same for any of the higher castes of Bali. Cremations are possibly the most photographed event of Balinese life. Many films of royal cremations have been made (the first in 1926) and are still being produced. We decided to add two further themes into the structure of the cremation rites.

The idea developed that we should attempt to show Lempad's unique life through his art and the changing times of Bali over the last hundred years in a manner similar to Balinese genealogical histories, called *babad*, which do their part in reinforcing the identity of the present generation by making them proud of their ancestors. A trip to Holland and New York provided us with some superb visual material to develop the historical themes. Much of this material has never been published and, in the case of the archival film, very seldom shown.

A slightly controversial aspect of our babad approach has been our use of the *tapel tua* (old man's mask) to represent Lempad's astral being. It is certainly used as a transitional cinematic technique and, as such, it successfully fulfils its purpose. However, there is more to it than just a cinematic trick. The *tapel tua* comes from *topeng*, which are the masked dance plays in which *babad* stories are told. Furthermore, this mask itself represents I Gusti Gauh Bale Dangin, who was an aged minister of the court of Gelgel in the 15th century. It is appropriate that the character on which the mask is based was a Gusti, the same caste as I Gusti Nyoman Lempad himself. In our film, the mask is filmed at the *merajan*, the temple for the ancestors of Lempad's family.

Of course for me, the most critical audience was my Balinese friends, particularly Lempad's family and the people of the village of Taman Kelod. One such screening remains in my memory. It was at the time of the family temple *odalan* (anniversary). The house courtyard was packed, the temple shrines finely decorated, the ancestral deities in attendance. The high priest who had officiated at Lempad's cremation, having completed his immediate rituals watched from his high stand. The film was viewed, in a way, as a shadow puppet performance for the living and the spiritual guests. It appeared to us that our work had passed its most stringent test.

I Gusti Made Sumung, Lempad's son, had an interesting response to the film. He told me that he was grateful that we had made the film as it provided a visual record for him and his family of those who had contributed their labour to making the cremation a success. Knowing this they would be able to repay the honour done to Lempad.

The film has been quite successful around the world, for which we are all grateful.

encounter

refracted in the eyes,
(like well springs)
of a quiet old man
once met
with grazing cow
and calf,
who
alone
at peace,
absorbed
in nature's rhythms,
slowly stared
far to the mountains
or deep into a flower;
was the light of a life lived
    pure.

pertemuan

terbiaskan di mata,
(bagai perigi)
seorang lelaki renta lembut
pernah jumpa
dengan sapi makan rumput
bersama anaknya,
yang
sendiri
damai,
hanyut
dalam irama semesta,
perlahan menatap
jauh ke pegunungan
atau ke lubuk sekuntum bunga;
adalah cahya kehidupan yang
    dijalankan suci.

Part II

Behind the Lens:
The Filmmaker and His Films

Introduction

Graeme MacRae

During the 1970s, John became known, especially in Australia, as the international go-to man for inside knowledge about Bali, and he advised and assisted a growing stream of journalists, academics and filmmakers. Among these were the brothers Lorne and Lawrence Blair, who made the acclaimed series *Ring of Fire* for British television.[1] Throughout this time, John saw himself primarily as a poet, but he was also practicing as an amateur ethnographer, exploring, discovering and documenting Balinese culture, especially its ritual and artistic dimensions. His career as a filmmaker was thrust upon him by circumstance rather than design, when his host and landlord, I Gusti Made Sumung, asked him to make a film of his father's cremation. John had never yet made a film.

With the cameraman and documentary filmmaker Lorne Blair, they began filming immediately, with no time for preparation, and over the following months they worked closely with Gusti Sumung to produce the film *Lempad of Bali*.[2] It was first screened on ABC Television (Australia) in 1980 and subsequently on a number of other television channels and at special events across the world. It also won the Mitra Award for Outstanding Planning at the 26th Asian Film Festival in Surabaya, where it was described as 'one of the festivals highlights' and 'one of the most moving film documents shown [...] in a long, long while'.³ Hildred Geertz, one of the senior anthropologists of Bali at the time, described it as 'a subtle and wise blending of historical information with exciting first-hand experience [...]. A poetic sensibility, a scholar's concern for accuracy and a deft understanding of Balinese life [...].'⁴

In *Lempad of Bali*, John established two methodological principles to which he returned in later films. One was that he 'attempted to tell the story from a Balinese p.o.v. [He] became familiar with the Balinese method of story-telling, particularly in the manner of telling history. They call it *babad*. It is a means by which elaboration turns historical facts into legend and myth.'⁵ The other was that, 'In the making of the film [he] relied on feedback from participants. [He] showed a preliminary rough cut to Lempad's family three times.' The Lempad family also owns a 10 percent equity of the film, from which they have received royalty payments ever since.

Lempad of Bali was an extraordinary achievement for a first film, even with the collaboration of an experienced filmmaker like Lorne Blair. John had found his medium and his path. He also realised at this point that film was another kind of poetry, and that in film, he had in a way found the voice he had been seeking in poetry. He began shooting footage and planning for other films as well as amassing a considerable body of research on Balinese life and culture, especially ritual. But he also realised that, in those pre-video days, film was a technically complex and expensive medium, so to make complete films, he had to find funding. The first opportunity came through a television series called *The Human Face of Indonesia*, funded by Film Australia and released in 1984. John worked as a location consultant on the entire series, and wrote and directed one episode, 'Master of the Shadows', about the Balinese master shadow puppeteer (*dalang*) Made Sija.

But he also embarked immediately on the opus magnum *Bali Triptych* – a summing up of his own understanding and interpretation of key aspects of Balinese culture. This was a labour of love in which he distilled and organised all the knowledge of Balinese culture that he had amassed in over a decade of immersion in everyday life, a systematic exploration of an encyclopaedic mass of information about the fundamental ritual basis of Balinese culture, brilliantly organised into a series of three one-hour films. The key to this complex organisation was a recently completed PhD thesis by the late Barbara Lovric.[6] *Bali Triptych* was shown on Australian television in 1988. The flavour of the reviews was similar to those for *Lempad of Bali*. Phillip Adams called it

> one of the most elegant, scholarly, and beautifully made documentary series you're likely to see [....] a series of such intensity, richness and privileged access into Balinese lives and rituals [...]. A cornucopia of cultural, spiritual and mystical richness.[7]

Viewed a quarter of a century later, what strikes me most about *Bali Triptych* is the documenting of the timeless quality of a way of life and ritual practice right at that moment when it was about to undergo its greatest transformation, due to tourism-driven development. This development was already evident at the time, but it is carefully excluded from *Bali Triptych*. It reads, in retrospect, as John's love-song and lament for a world loved and lost, and indeed it was his own swan-song in Bali. He left soon afterwards, citing the changes as one of his reasons.

Another concurrent project, the series *Slow Boat from Surabaya* was shown on ABC, BBC and PBS television in late 1988. John was again location producer for the whole series, and writer/director of an episode called 'The Five Faces of God', which was about religious diversity in Indonesia. Together, these projects cemented his place as the prime foreign filmmaker of Indonesia. It was said that 'you don't make a film in Indonesia without talking to John Darling'.[8]

Sadly, he developed deepening problems with his health. He was also disillusioned with changes in Bali and in his own life, including his separation from Diana, and he had already returned to Australia. He kept planning films and looking for funding, as well as establishing his own production company Taman Sari Productions, named, like his *pondok*, after a beautiful old temple at the heart of the neighbourhood where he lived in Ubud. Taman Sari's first production was *Bali Hash*, an ethnographically innovative film edited out of some of his existing footage, juxtaposing the bizarre excesses of the Hash House Harriers with (more exotic but arguably less bizarre) Balinese ritual. It too was first released on Australian television, in 1989.[9] Stylistically, it was a change of direction from his previous work and signalled a more culturally critical approach. This direction is evident in proposals for several films which never came to fruition, including Indian Cricket (1988), Golf Bali (1991) and Kampung Cowboys (1986), a retelling of the Mahabharata story through a group of young Balinese men.

Despite his stature as an established filmmaker, his first years back in Australia between 1987 and the early 1990s were characterised by loss of personal direction and artistic frustration. As well as the unrealised proposals noted above, others included films on high-achieving young Australians (Young People: Young Country, 1986), the Indian Ocean (West of Perth), and the eccentric Australian painter Ian Fairweather.

A breakthrough came in 1992 when he obtained funding from the Australian Broadcasting Commission for a film about traditional

Introduction

seafarers in eastern Indonesia and their links with northern Australia. In 1993 he spent eleven weeks filming, and the resulting film, *Below the Wind*, was first screened on ABC Television in January 1994; it then aired on television in several other countries as well as screening at festivals. The reviews were similar to those of his previous films: *The Age* called it a 'superbly crafted and detailed documentary', and *In the Picture* described it as 'ABC's most interesting Indonesia-related broadcast of recent years and Darling's best work to date.'[10]

Through the rest of the 1990s, John's health prevented further film projects, but he continued to act as a consultant for others, as well as teaching documentary filmmaking at Murdoch University. But the catastrophic Kuta bombings in October 2002 motivated him to film again despite his health. With his wife Sara as co-producer, nurse and production manager, he moved to Bali for several months to film *The Healing of Bali*. The film premiered on Australian television on the first anniversary of the bombings. It was to be his last film, as his health problems limited his ability to travel and work.

While John's films were ostensibly about Indonesia, they were addressed to Australian viewers and most of them had at least a subtext of Indonesia's relationship with Australia. But John was deeply Australian and he had long wanted to make films more directly about his own country, so after the success of *The Healing of Bali* he began preparations for a new film, to be called *Bleaching Australia*. Together with his distributor, Ronin Films, he applied for funding, enough of which was granted to make a start. It began as a relatively straightforward documentary about the 'History Wars' which were convulsing Australian intellectual life at the time,[11] but it soon developed into something more complex. Reflexive and ambitious, it involved a lot of Indigenous voices, John's own family history,

Western District history, and Geelong Grammar, and had an extensive online database of 'footnotes' and archival material documenting the evidence on which the film is based. It was to be a film about Australian history and the way it is represented, but ultimately it was also about national identity. But, despite a large amount of research and the production of a short sample for fundraising purposes, it never got any further because of John's failing health. It might have been a new direction for John – into Australian cinema and public debate. Instead he redirected his artistic impulses to the less physically demanding medium of painting.

His film legacy lives on in the John Darling Fellowship, established in 2013 to support exchange visits of young filmmakers between Australia and Indonesia. Since 2018 the focus has shifted to providing opportunities for young Australian filmmakers to travel, study, work and exchange ideas in Indonesia.[12]

John never systematically articulated his philosophy and approach to filmmaking, but he did talk about it a lot and there are glimpses of it in his writings. Where we perhaps get closest to these ideas is in his (voluminous but fragmented) notes for his lectures and talks at Murdoch University, where he taught a course on documentary film from 1990 till 1995.

His primary text for teaching film was Crawford and Turton's *Film as Ethnography*,[13] which was at the time a new and important work on ethnographic film. Among the films he showed his students were *State of Shock* (David Bradbury), *The Times of Harvey Milk* (Gus van Sant), *Rosie the Riveter* (Connie Field), *Jaguar*, *Les Maîtres Fous* (Jean Rouch), *Wittgenstein* (Derek Jarman), *Gimme Shelter* (the Maysles brothers), *Don't look Back* (D. A. Pennebaker), *The Ax Fight* (Timothy Asch), the Jero Tapakan series (Timothy and Patsy Asch and Linda

Connor), *Trobriand Cricket* (Gary Kildea), *Night Mail* (Harry Watt and Basil Wright), *Nanook of the North* (Robert Flaherty), and *First Contact* (Bob Connolly). Most of these are classics of documentary, but some are also classics of ethnographic film.

John's approach to filmmaking can perhaps best be summed up in his own words:

> Within the tradition of documentary film I call myself an ethnographic filmmaker. By that I mean [...] I collect ethnographic data which I then collate and edit into a virtual reality of what actually happened. [...] In the words of Gregory Bateson, [...] I am looking for 'those patterns that connect' [...] the camera must be knowledgeable and intelligent, and must act as one of the participants of the event [...] being filmed. The filmmaker should have the fullest support of the people about whom the film concerns. [...] The challenge is to tell other peoples' stories in a manner which is both culturally acceptable to them and [...] understandable to other people beyond those cultural boundaries.
>
> [...] the camera as an impartial observer seems to me to be the easy way out, of not having researched and understood your culture and [...] subject matter.
>
> [...] the filmmaker should do the best possible to thoroughly understand people the film is [...] about by spending considerable time on location and [...] gaining their confidence and understanding before he begins filming. The filmmaker should do his best to let the Indigenous structure of events act as the guide in the editing of the final film.
>
> I see filmmaking as nothing more or less than storytelling. The gift of good filmmakers in [...] documentary [...] is being clear about the story they want to tell. [...]. The story should [...] be told in compelling pictures – the words only adding insights and explanation where absolutely necessary.

My particular interests [... include the ...] dangerous edge between cultures – between tradition and technological progress. I attempted it with *Bali Hash*, but I wish to go a lot further.

[...] You must make the person or people you are making your film about think of it as their film [...] you have made a moral contract with them.

It's all about your voice – in the poet's sense – I've found it in poetry in its truest sense – occasionally in films.

In the next four chapters, David Hanan discusses John's main films in more detail; Sara Darling tells the story of the making of *The Healing of Bali*; Douglas Lewis reflects on some of the implications of *Lempad of Bali*; and Toby Miller moves between the man and the filmmaker.

Notes

1. See https://www.drlawrenceblair.com/films.
2. For more detail on the making of *Lempad of Bali*, see John's own account in Part I of this book.
3. *The Hollywood Reporter*, 8 July 1980; Joe Quiriro, *Asiaweek*, 25 July 1980.
4. Hildred Geertz, 'A letter of recommendation to prospective funders for Bali Triptych', 15 September 1982, John Darling collection.
5. John's own words, from one of his lectures at Murdoch University in the 1990s.
6. Barbara Lovric, *Rhetoric and Reality: The Hidden Nightmare–Myth and Magic as Representations of Morbid Realities*, unpublished doctoral thesis, University of Sydney, 1987. Personal communication from Helen Simons, 2021.
7. Phillip Adams, The Weekend Australian, 17–18 September 1988. See also Janet Hawley, The Sydney Morning Herald, 19 September 1988.
8. Diana Simmonds, *The Sydney Morning Herald*, 10 October 1988.
9. The Hash House Harriers are an international network of expatriate clubs devoted to cross-country running and the consumption of beer.
10. Richard Plunkett, 'Seafarers' Plight Superbly Told', *The Age*, 6 January 1994; Krishna Sen, *In the Picture*, Winter 1994.
11. The History Wars were a hotly contested debate over competing interpretations of the colonisation of Australia and its effects on Indigenous peoples and subsequent Australian understandings of the past. A key

account is Stuart and Anna Macintyre, *The History Wars* (Carlton, Victoria: Melbourne University Publishing, 2003).
12 See https://www.acicis.edu.au/programs/practicum/creative-arts-and-design-professional-practicum-cadpp/john-darling-fellowship/.
13 Peter Ian Crawford and David Turton, eds. *Film as Ethnography* (Manchester: Manchester University Press in association with the Granada Centre for Visual Anthropology, 1992).

Encountering Bali, and Other Indonesian Societies, through Filmmaking

David Hanan

One of Australia's most significant filmmakers to work in Southeast Asia was John Darling (1946–2011), who made Bali his home during the 1970s and 1980s. Although initially he thought of himself primarily as a poet, over the next decade he served as a cultural consultant to filmmakers working in Bali, and in 1978 began work on his first film, on the life and death of the Balinese architect, sculptor and painter, I Gusti Nyoman Lempad. Together, the film *Lempad of Bali* and five other documentary films John made about Bali constitute the most important single body of filmmaking about Bali to date. This essay commemorates John by exploring all of the films that he personally wrote, produced and directed.

After graduating from the Australian National University, John travelled to the UK to commence postgraduate work in British history at Oxford University. On a return visit to Australia he stopped over in Kuala Lumpur and travelled to Jakarta and then on to Bali. In Malaysia and Indonesia, John immediately felt stimulated by, and temperamentally suited to, Southeast Asia. He abandoned his postgraduate research in the UK and moved to Bali, briefly living in Kuta and then in Ubud, where he lived for some time in a simple hut (*pondok*) with an earthen floor.

During this time, John also explored other parts of Indonesia. In 1972, he undertook a sea voyage on local boats to islands in eastern Indonesia, where he was shipwrecked and marooned for some weeks. He had important encounters with seafaring and fishing peoples, who in the early 1990s became the subject of his documentary *Below the Wind*. Over time, John developed enough fluency in both Balinese and Indonesian to make connections with local people. His films reflect his deep interest in and understanding of the many Balinese ceremonies, rituals and related performance forms, which he aims to present as much as possible from the point of view of the Balinese, seeking detailed advice on their meaning, and recording them and explaining them in great detail in his films. The last film John made was *The Healing of Bali*, an encounter with Balinese victims of the infamous Bali bombing of October 2002.

In tone, John's films vary from the reverential, indeed sublime, *Lempad of Bali*, to the eye-opening exposé *Below the Wind*, with its prescient account of the treatment of Rotinese fishermen by Australian maritime and immigration authorities, to the irreverent and humorous *Bali Hash*, with its wry cultural comparisons between western Hash Harrier expatriates, and the culturally sophisticated Balinese.

I knew John, and we saw each other as friends with similar interests and cultural intuitions even though the number of times we actually met was relatively few. After his long sojourn in Bali, he lived in Perth, then Canberra, Melbourne and finally Perth again for the last years of his life, but his increasing exhaustion from his blood disease limited his capacity for social interaction. On those occasions when we did meet, at conferences in Canberra or on his visits to Melbourne, there was an immediate sense of shared experience and common assumptions, which resulted in long and engaging conversations. I think many people, particularly those who travelled in Indonesia and thought about the country, experienced this with John.

What follows is a discussion of John's main films, in chronological order.

Lempad of Bali (1980)

I Gusti Nyoman Lempad was a Balinese sculptor, architect and painter who moved to Ubud as a young man in the late nineteenth century due to political circumstances facing his father. He subsequently created many of the finest palaces, temple gates and carved monuments in Ubud. Among these was the temple Pura Taman Kumuda Saraswati, dedicated to the goddess of wisdom, science and the arts, built in the 1950s after Indonesia won independence. He also contributed to the building of the Museum Puri Lukisan, now known for its extensive collection of Balinese painting and sculpture.

Estimated to have been born in 1862, Lempad, who was a highly spiritual and, by all reports, an exceedingly modest person, died on 25 April 1978 at the remarkable age of 116 years. Lempad's paintings and drawings were particularly distinctive and accomplished at a time of new developments in Balinese painting, which were partly stimulated by new materials and production methods introduced by the European painters Rudolf Bonnet and Walter Spies from the late 1920s onwards. Many of Lempad's drawings and paintings from this period, some depicting scenes from Balinese legends, have mythological and subtly erotic themes. They are distinctive for their bold lines and a combination of elegance and quirky humour. In a review of the sumptuous book on Lempad's art recently published by the Museum Puri Lukisan, *Lempad of Bali* (to which John Darling contributed), Hildred Geertz distinguishes Lempad's work on paper from that of his innovative Balinese contemporaries in the 1930s, who filled the picture plane with bright colours, remarking that Lempad's 'line drawings in black ink and his distinctive energetic line were never imitated' (Geertz, 2015).

Although it was John's first film, *Lempad of Bali* (produced and directed with Lorne Blair as cameraman) is a subtle, sophisticated and intricate film that interweaves numerous strands and threads of Lempad's life in ways that illuminate much about Bali. The aged Lempad himself is seen only briefly, early in the film, in footage shot by Lorne Blair in 1977, where he comments that he had been re-incarnated to serve the gods by creating works of art. The film's thematic exposition, commencing with Lempad's death, is multilayered in its approach to narrative and time. First, it provides a portrait of the artist himself, showing both his life and his evolving works; second, it locates him in the context of Balinese history from the 1860s; third, in its portrait of an exceptionally old man (and his spirituality), it is suggestive of the mystery of life itself, and of evolving spiritual potentialities over time; and fourth, it is a study of Balinese funerary rituals and their relation to the deceased individual and to his family. At numerous points, strikingly original paintings by Lempad are used to illustrate the spiritual and material themes explored in the film.

Lempad's life spanned a transition in Balinese art from a time when most art was religious and anonymous to the arrival and influence of Western artists, who, while respecting Balinese religion and culture, brought with them a greater emphasis on individual creativity. In so far as the film is a portrait of an exceptional artist, it also emphasises Lempad's relation to his community, and the relation of his art to his community's beliefs and values.

John's later three-part film, *Bali Triptych*, presents a comprehensive, indeed encyclopaedic overview of numerous Balinese ceremonies. On the other hand, *Lempad of Bali*, which begins with Lempad's death and then interweaves his life story with preparations for his funeral – culminating with his cremation ceremony and concluding with the scattering of his ashes into the sea – presents a sense of what it is for an individual and for his family to be part of these ceremonies. In this sense the ceremonies, and the respect they show for both the living and the recently departed Lempad, are more personalised than the ceremonies explained in *Bali Triptych*, both in their contextualisation of Lempad's life and in the meaning they hold for his surviving close relatives.[1]

At the same time as the film develops a very personal set of relationships to Balinese ceremonies, and to one family, it also contextualises Lempad's long life in the events that surrounded him. Lempad was born at a time of numerous factional wars in Bali and only a decade or so after the rebellion by I Gusti Ketut Jelantik against increasing Dutch incursions into North Bali. He died in the decade of man's first landing on the moon – the same decade that saw the introduction of mass tourism into Bali.

Another thread in the film is the tripartite distinction between body, soul and astral being, the latter two constituting the eternal elements of the self that continue in future incarnations. As the narrator remarks, the Balinese believe in reincarnation, and regard an individual life as 'no more than one adventure in a continuous cycle of incarnation'. Quite early in the film, Lempad's son, I Gusti Made Sumung, explains how the use of a white cloth for the wrapping of the body after death is a symbol for the way the soul and astral being are held together, via the uniting of the various *chakras* – a Sanskrit term for the various centres of spiritual power in the body – thus facilitating the spiritual journey into the underworld. The transpersonal 'astral being' is symbolised by various means in a number of the ceremonies shown in the film (at one point, by a mask; at another by a long white pole linked by a red symbolic umbilical cord to a soul, which is cradled like a baby). Later in the film we learn that the aged Lempad spent the last years of his life mainly in meditation, but also in carving a mask, the face of 'a young soul', to which he would return at the time of his reincarnation (see image no. 11). The film thus invokes for the viewer the way in which Balinese life can be lived, not only by intimations of mortality, but of a hypothesised spiritual world, made up of ancestors and also of new spiritual potentials.

John initially saw himself as a poet rather than a filmmaker, and his poetic instincts show themselves in the imagery at key moments in his films, and in the sound.[2] The opening shots of *Lempad of Bali*, of rice fields in the half light of dawn, or of sunset – the exquisitely sculptured fields half buried in shadows of their valleys, with a man and perhaps a boy silhouetted in the far distance – are full of metaphoric implications that resonate with the themes of the film: the shape of a life in a material world, and the continuing journey of the soul through numerous incarnations via a spirit world. Transitions in the film are sometimes marked by the distinctive, barely audible presence of a sacred bell. At the end of the film, as the family gathers again on the seashore at Lebih, where Lempad's ashes had been dispersed ten days earlier, the men in boats off shore, appear and disappear behind the rising and falling waves. This concluding shot, of humans appearing and disappearing in the ocean, is held, lingering, until a final fade out and the transition to a still photograph of Lempad's family, acknowledging their involvement in the making of the film.

Indeed the film was made primarily at the suggestion of Lempad's own son, I Gusti Made Sumung, who frequently acts as a commentator within the film, and who had been, as a young man, interpreter and advisor to the American anthropologist Jane Belo and others researching in Bali in the 1930s.[3]

* * *

Lempad's life is presented as comprising distinct periods, each differing in both creativity and spiritual condition. Lempad initially worked in Ubud, primarily as an architect, sculptor and builder of palaces. The arrival of the Dutch in southern Bali in 1906 was exceptionally traumatic, with the suicide of the Denpasar royal family in the face of Dutch guns. However, the gradual influx of European artists in the 1920s led to a renaissance in Balinese art in the 1930s, in which Lempad took part. Balinese artists began to paint on paper and to show an interest in contemporary subjects rather than only traditional mythological themes. Then, during the Japanese occupation in the early 1940s, Lempad withdrew into himself. He was in deep meditation, almost catatonic, his family and friends report. But following the Dutch transfer of sovereignty at the end of 1949, Lempad, at the age of ninety, embarked on a new period of creativity in the early 1950s. This last creative period, the film argues, drew on imagery from his earliest experiences as a child, living near the remains of a 10th-century monastery, and also from the remarkable 14th-century rock carvings at Yeh Pulu, near his family's original rice fields in Bedulu. These robust carvings of daily life, which in popular mythology are regarded as the work of a giant, are thought by experts to be the work of one person because of their distinctiveness and stylistic coherence.

But the film does not concentrate solely on the evolution of this unique artist and on the history of art and architecture in the region. Significant sequences show the numerous ways Lempad's family and fellow villagers, including his surviving second wife and other women, are involved, as a tightly knit community, in the various funeral rituals over the six-week period between Lempad's death and his cremation. The narrator points out that the arts and crafts involved in preparing and carrying out the cremation rituals provide a framework for all of Lempad's associates to contribute their various skills, building, for example, the funeral tower which transports the body to the cremation site, as well as the cremation bull itself, in which the body is burned. Yet both the cremation tower and the bull will later be consumed by fire, for Balinese rituals recognise the fundamental transience of all things human.

Balinese community assumptions, values and practices are exemplified in the film in other ways. Two values are explicitly mentioned in the depiction of the funeral rites. First there is the ritual, shown very early in the film, of the washing of the corpse by those closest to the deceased; as the narrator comments, the Western use of professionals to perform the task of preparing the body for burial are seen by the Balinese as barbaric. Second, invitations to Lempad's cremation, particularly to important members of the community, are made by personal visits rather than in print form. This is seen by the Balinese as much more respectful, and is accompanied by a gift of food.

Bali Triptych: Three Films about the History, Culture and Way of Life of the People of Bali (1988)

John Darling's second major film, *Bali Triptych*, is an unusually densely populated documentary, rich in colourful imagery and exceptionally detailed information about Balinese traditions and history. Indeed the film was almost certainly conceived as a way of introducing viewers – in as comprehensive and dynamic a way possible – to a fuller understanding of the world in which Lempad lived. John Darling himself had discovered this world in the 1970s, and he wanted to share it with foreign viewers who have some sense of the beauty of Bali and its customs and traditions, but little understanding of the complexity of its traditions or its social organisation.

This nearly three-hour film is in three parts, hence its title. In the history of art, particularly European art, it is common for a triptych to have a religious theme, to deal with different aspects of the same subject, and to be filled with rich detail. The metaphor of a triptych for a three part, three-hour film, is apt, in that it presents a detailed and comprehensive picture, in three phases, of the Balinese universe. The documentation in the film is encyclopaedic, almost scientific in tone, in its relatively impersonal exposition, even when dealing with mythological subjects.

Each of the three parts deals with a different aspect of Bali. Episode I, 'Between Mountain and Sea', provides an account of Balinese history, starting with the origins of the island in volcanic eruptions millions of years ago; the arrival of rice-cultivating peoples from mainland Asia (and the nature of the agricultural methods they developed in Bali); and the coming of Indian influences at around 700 AD. Later sections of Episode I outline, in a more systematic way than in the Lempad film, the history of modern Bali, beginning with the first European contacts at the time of Sir Francis Drake, followed by the gradual subjection of Bali to Dutch colonialism in the latter part of the 19th and early 20th centuries, and the Japanese occupation during the Second World War. Episode I concludes with the emergence of tourist Bali in the context of an independent Indonesia, with its troubled political history.

Episode II, 'The Path of the Soul', establishes a rather different set of preoccupations, and uses different methods. It is entirely devoted to an exhaustive account of the ceremonies which a Balinese person will experience, from birth to death, and the meaning and role of these ceremonies for the community and the individual. Episode II has a relatively clear linear structure, outlining step by step the rituals that provide a path for the soul from five months into pregnancy, through birth, childhood, marriage and so on, to the final funeral. The film, for the most part, documents real rituals, rather than staging re-enactments.

Episode III, 'Demons and Deities', continues the preoccupations with traditional rituals, however not those held within a family for an individual, but with more spectacular events, involving whole communities and large groups. These could be mass trance communication with deities, the ten-day joint festivals *Galungan* and *Kuningan* which celebrate the visits of gods and family ancestors to earth and their return, or mass rituals of exorcism.

While much of the film concentrates on spiritual beliefs and the mythological figures and rituals associated with them, fundamental material aspects of Balinese society are addressed in a lengthy section half way through Episode I, which provides a systematic introduction to the major mode of production in Bali, the long-evolved systems for cultivating rice. This central section outlines the processes involved in the growing and harvesting of rice, and the division of labour between men and women. While men plough the fields, and plant and cultivate the rice, women transplant seedlings, harvest and thresh the rice, and are the principal buyers and sellers at markets. The section begins with an account of the irrigation system in Bali, asserting that the sustained availability of water for rice cultivation comes from a system of channels or canals that feed the water from volcanic lakes such as Lake Batur, high in the mountains. This extensive irrigation system is maintained by village cooperatives, known as *subak*, an organisation dating back at least a thousand years, with long fostered skills in developing irrigation systems and negotiating agreements about distributing the water among communities. Rice itself, like anything central to Balinese life, is invested with sacred properties, and as a result ceremonies surround its planting and cultivation, and the *subak* organisation itself has links with water-temples. The narrator summarises the factors that have benefited rice-growing in Bali and made it central to the economy: the volcanic soil, a long and successful agricultural tradition, the *subak* system of irrigation, and disease-resistant strains of rice.

Episode II of the triptych, 'The Path of the Soul', while showing a wide variety of ceremonies, argues that the basic religious and cultural presupposition of a Balinese person is that when a baby is born, they are the re-incarnation of an ancestor, who may be of either gender. The numerous ceremonies and rites relate to the protection of this ancestral spirit and of the young child, even as a foetus. Moments of transition – such as birth or the release of the soul at death, when the gateway between this world and the supernatural realm of the ancestors is forced open – are regarded as particularly dangerous. The narrator comments that Balinese rituals consist of complex prescriptions and rules of avoidance to allay the dangerous spirits in the environment, seen for example in the numerous temple offerings. An early ritual in

Episode II shows a family with a spirit medium at a séance where they seek to determine which ancestor is reincarnated in a newborn child.

In presenting his exposition, particularly on the ceremonies and prescriptions surrounding infancy, Darling draws on the work of Gregory Bateson and Margaret Mead, who did anthropological work in Bali in the late 1930s. Citing their argument that Balinese character is based upon a fear of transgressing divine rules by neglecting the supernatural dimensions of their world, this fear is balanced by the assuredness the Balinese hold in their social position and duties. 'The Path of the Soul' is particularly detailed in presenting the numerous ceremonies and prescriptions related to birth and the early months of the child's life. However, some of these ceremonies and prescriptions appear to be determined not solely by a sense of obligations to the spirit world, but embody other kinds of values. For example, following a child's birth, both parents – at least in villages at the time the film was made – are confined to the house for a period of three days. As well, the child in infancy is mainly carried on the hip and not allowed to crawl on the ground. Indeed there is a ceremony held 105 days (three Balinese 'months') after birth, when the young child's feet are first allowed to touch the ground. While the film comments that 'crawling' is regarded by the Balinese as an attribute of animals, not worthy of a re-incarnated ancestral soul, the fact that the child is carried on the hip for much of its infancy, whether by a parent, or by an elder sibling, increases the child's closeness and identification with its family and community group. This point was emphasised by Bateson and Mead in their discussion of kinaesthetic learning, in their pioneering work of visual anthropology, published in 1942, *Balinese Character: A Photographic Analysis* (Bateson and Mead, 1942). It was developed at greater length by Mead in *Growth and Culture* (Mead and Macgregor, 1950: 41–50). Bateson and Mead not only explored child-rearing practices of the Balinese but also correlated principles they had isolated in these practices with structures discernible in dances and ceremonies, thus attempting to locate their meanings deep within Balinese culture. These arguments were presented not only in their original book but also in later writings by Bateson (Bateson, 2000).

John Darling incorporates shots by Bateson and Mead into his film, as well as stills from their photographic study of Balinese character. His commentary also makes use of some of Bateson and Mead's insights, for example in his discussion of the *joged* dance as community ritual. While now a well-known dance performed for tourists, it was originally an interactive, socialising dance organised for Balinese teenagers by the village elders, described in the film as 'a community commissioned flirtatious dance performance'. Episode III of the film, 'Demons and Deities', also makes use of footage and insights developed by Bateson and Mead, particularly in the sections exploring cockfighting and temple-based trance dances, including dances involving exorcism.

Both *Lempad of Bali* and *Bali Triptych* (especially Episode I) make effective use of still photographs and actual footage from earlier eras; particularly memorable are photographs of the Dutch invasion of South Bali in September 1906. This culminated in the *puputan* (mass suicide) of almost the entire royal family of Badung (Denpasar), totalling some 600 people, who immolated themselves and their families, as they marched in protest out of their royal compound in the face of Dutch guns, hence demonstrating their deep commitment to Balinese autonomy. In the 21st century, tourists, searching for the nearby Australian consulate, or making the journey by taxi from Sanur to Denpasar, rarely know the origins of the name of the street on which they are travelling, Jalan Puputan Raya, but Darling brings home the importance of this – and other *puputan* – at the time of the subjugation of Bali by the colonising Dutch. Episode II culminates in a remarkable, dynamically filmed, fifteen-minute sequence showing the final path of a soul, including the huge funeral – and all its attendant preparations and rituals, climaxing in the cremation – held on 17 March 1986, of Cokorda Gede Ngurah Pemecutan; known as the 'King of Denpasar', as a young boy he was reputedly the sole survivor of the royal family of Badung in the *puputan* of 1906.

Bali Triptych is a film dazzling in the richness, colour and detail with which its subject is presented. Indeed it exemplifies, through auditory and visual means, the remarks of the narrator about Balinese ceremonies as a whole, made early in Part II: 'Balinese rites encapsulate a blend of sophistication and simplicity, vibrancy and eeriness: they engage all the senses'. Perhaps it is this that made one scholar casually remark to me that John's films are to a degree 'orientalist'. Certainly I would agree they are exotic, but only in the way that Bali is exotic. Edward Said, whose discussion of orientalism, in effect, gave modern definition to the term 'orientalist', has himself indicated in an 'Afterword' to a later edition of his seminal book that notions of cultural difference (and hence, we may say, exoticism) were not in themselves the object of his critique (Said, 1995, 352). Rather, for Said, it was the view that underlay many discourses of 'the other', the different and the exotic – to the effect that exotic societies were primitive and hence inferior – that needed to be critiqued. John Darling's films, on the contrary, marvel at Balinese civilisation, finding it deeply intriguing and something to be understood. He does not regard it as an inferior civilisation, and so gives it as detailed and intricate a coverage as possible, so much so that he provides a picture that some viewers have described as overwhelming.

All three episodes of *Bali Triptych* emphasise traditional ceremonies, rituals and rites. There are, of course, other aspects of Bali that might well also have been addressed. One is the particular forms of local community organisation and debate, as seen in the *banjar* (the hamlet, its boundaries forming a local customary, or sometimes government administrative unit). This aspect of Bali has been explored in considerable detail, for example in Carol Warren's excellent study, *Adat and Dinas: Balinese Communities in the Indonesian State* (Warren, 1993). Darling does draw on one aspect of Warren's work in his depiction of the *subak* – the institutional means by which communities agree upon, establish and maintain irrigation systems in a democratic spirit. How Balinese communities organise themselves around ongoing contemporary social issues, and the institutions for doing this, could have been the subject of a whole other documentary, presenting an even more varied and comprehensive view of Balinese life than that presented in *Bali Triptych*. Nevertheless, Darling does engage pertinently at times with other aspects of Balinese community organisation, both directly and by implication, in his subsequent films about Bali, *Bali Hash* and *The Healing of Bali*.

Given its very comprehensive investigation of Balinese history and the ceremonial aspects of the society, *Bali Triptych* would benefit from being published as an e-book, as has already occurred with *Lempad of Bali*. While John Darling himself could not be the author, such a book could then consist – in addition to the film – of the text of the narration of each of the three episodes, together with accompanying photographs, so that the reader could contemplate the arguments and evidence of this rich, yet densely argued film, without being hindered by the way all films inevitably impose their own continuous and unrelenting time on the viewer.

Bali Hash (1989)

> 'If you have half a mind to join the Hash, that's all you need.'
> (Statement by the Inter-Hash Grand Master at the conclusion of *Bali Hash*)

Bali Hash is a film about the three-day 'InterHash' held in Bali by the International Hash House Harriers, in 1988. Hash Harriers engage in weekly runs for health and recreational reasons, meet regularly for dinners, and also hold beer drinking festivals and a biennial international get-together. The organisation was founded by English expatriates in Kuala Lumpur, Malaya, during the late colonial period, in 1938. The term 'hash' derives from the word for the (largely disliked) institutional food served in English public schools and also in the British army, and had a connection with the initial dining venue for the Harriers in Kuala Lumpur. Over the post-war years, the highly masculinist Hash Harriers have internationalised. By 1988 membership was no longer restricted to male expatriates: the organisation now included Asian businessmen – and even women, known as 'Harriettes'. The 1988 International Hash held in Bali had some 3,000 participants from more than 700 clubs in some 75 countries, although the organisation saw itself as still primarily Southeast Asian.

The 1988 Bali Inter-Hash coincided with the Balinese holiday Galungan, one of the most important religious events in the Balinese 210-day annual calendar. It is a time when the deified ancestors are said to return to earth, with extensive ceremonies, decorations and festivities welcoming them. It is also said to celebrate the victory of *dharma* (order) over chaos (*adharma*). This island-wide festival continues until Kuningan, ten days later, when the gods return to their celestial regions. John's film, co-directed with Australian documentary filmmaker John Moyle, doesn't only explores the spectacle of the Inter-Hash; it cuts between the Inter-Hash events and the Galungan festivities and rituals, thus producing an ironically humorous cultural contrast between the rituals and festivities of the Hash House Harriers, and those of the Balinese.

Opening with a gong and striking images of Balinese masks and carvings, *Bali Hash* quickly creates a contrast between these images and the activities of the Hash House Harriers, beginning with the raucous singing of some Western women about the values of Bintang beer, on a stage set for the entertainment of the variously – sometimes obscenely – clad beer-drinking harriers. The film then cuts to confusion in the office of the Harriers Hospitality Administrative Centre as they attempt to cope with the many complications arising from the arrival of guests from all over the globe. Here the character of the somewhat harassed grand master of the Inter-Hash, Victor Mason, is established, providing a sympathetic point of entry into the Harriers. There are interviews with individual Harriers, and with groups, in which the characteristics of their 'culture' are explored. One fundamental and constantly recurring Hash ritual is the 'down-down', where, as punishment – sometimes for success and sometimes for failure – individual Harriers are required to down two and a half litres of beer in one go, with minimal spillage, the event being adjudicated by marshals. Eventually the film cuts away to the Balinese soberly preparing their colourful Galungan rituals, the decorations of which 'turn the whole island into a temple'.

From its opening moments, *Bali Hash* has a particular narrative tone. In contrast to the decorous and quietly respectful voice-over accompanying John Darling's earlier films about Bali, the *Bali Hash* narration is bemused and worldly-wise. While the film maintains this ironic perspective throughout, the situation on the ground is leavened by the tolerant attitudes of the Balinese, who, in keeping with their customary hospitality, ensure that all required facilities are available for their overseas visitors. Indeed the Inter-Hash is declared open by a baffled but respectful Balinese government official, a gamelan orchestra and dancers, along with an *ogoh-ogoh* (paper mâché giant designed to scare away demons), and the event is blessed by Balinese women bearing incense, before the *ogoh-ogoh* is set alight.

The film might also be seen as an extended metaphor as to how the Balinese cope with the excesses of tourism in general, and indeed early in the film there is a section soberly exploring the impact of tourism since the opening of the international airport at Denpasar in 1969. Here various Balinese comment on the financial benefits of tourism for Balinese society as a whole, and the capacity of Balinese culture to resist the invasion of very different value systems and models of behaviour.

While providing much information both about the Hash House Harriers and Balinese festivals, is in its structure *Bali Hash* is almost a parody of commonly found documentary organisational methods. For example, while the first part of the film sets up a sardonic contrast between the Balinese and the Hash House Harriers, its concluding moments draw similarities between the Hash Harriers and the Balinese: at one point it argues that many of the rituals of both Balinese and the Harriers are cathartic in nature; then later, it shows village men celebrating their rice harvest by drinking *tuak* (palm wine) and singing – with glittering eyes, considerable camaraderie, and a high degree of inebriation – their songs imitating the sounds of frogs and birds. The narrator goes on to claim, tongue in cheek, that for the Balinese, drinking alcohol is a means of placating and driving away demons, and in that sense, the activities of the Hash House Harriers, who consumed 65,000 cans of beer in their three-day festival, were doing the Balinese a service. The film thus goes back on its original premise, in effect undermining the cultural contrast earlier presented, by producing deliberately platitudinous generalisations with the narrator quietly mocking his own arguments as he presents them. In its concluding sections the film, with deliberate irony, conforms to the tendency of more conventional documentaries to attempt to fulfil all possible audience expectations and seek a resolution, by introducing a core Balinese value, namely harmony between all the participants.

Below the Wind (1994)

The only film outside of Bali that John Darling wrote and directed himself is about the Sama Bajo people of Sulawesi Tenggara (Southeast Sulawesi), who for some hundreds of years have fished in waters they refer to as 'below the wind', that is to say, north of Australia, between Australia and Timor and between Arnhem Land and New Guinea.[4]

As the film shows, these early visits by the Sama Bajo, and later by Makassarese, led to more sustained contact with Aboriginal people, including intermarriage over hundreds of years, recorded in Aboriginal songs and stories, and even in their body painting.

Below the Wind is a portrait both of a people and their means of livelihood. It is also raises justice and human-rights issues with regard to the treatment of the Sama Bajo fishermen by the Australian government. Traditionally the Sama Bajo have fished for trepang, shark fin, turtle shell, trochus shell and reef fish in the Timor and Arafura seas. Since 1979, with the extension of the Australian claim of exclusive fishing rights to 200 nautical miles beyond the Australian shoreline, the Sama Bajo, who previously had fished legally to twelve nautical miles off Australia, have been subject to the threat of being arrested, and fined or imprisoned, their boats confiscated and burnt, if they are found fishing in what are now – under Australian law – regarded as Australian territorial waters. The film opens with an Australian Defence Force patrol boat bailing up one of these fishing boats, firing warning shots, and hailing the crew in Australian English with a loudspeaker. After their arrest, the fishermen are read, in English legalese, the regulations under which they are to be incarcerated.[5]

The central sections of the film begin with a lengthy sequence showing a core settlement of the Sama Bajo living in houses built over the water on shorelines. These are in isolated areas of Sulawesi Tenggara where 300,000 Sama Bajo live – amounting to some 25% of the total population of this nomadic people, who are spread throughout the Southern Philippines and Eastern Indonesia. The film documents their traditional rituals and the fragile nature of the economies that support these communities. It shows that due to their nomadic way of life, the Sama Bajo remain marginalised, never officially recognised by the Indonesian government as a genuine *suku* (distinct ethnic group). Thus they have very little formal education; the majority were still illiterate in 1993 when the film was shot. One group of Sama Bajo live their lives entirely on boats, often shifting location depending on the availability of fish.

The film's voice-over is spoken by John Darling himself. He states early on that he first encountered the Sama Bajo people in 1972, when he was stranded for three weeks after a shipwreck on a small island in the Flores Sea. It was then that he first heard of Sama Bajo voyages to Australia, and, as he states: 'their resourceful and dignified way of life impressed me then, and determined my resolve to find out more about the sea nomads of Indonesia'. Visually *Below the Wind* is distinctive, large sections of it filmed on the sailing boats used by these people, or along the green and blue, seemingly pristine, shoreline waters of Southeast Sulawesi, or the white sands of Rote island, where recently migrated Sama Bajo communities live.

The fishermen from the Sama Bajo communities sell their produce to a small group of Chinese Indonesian entrepreneurs based in Makassar, who specialise particularly in trading in highly valued shark fin, trochus shells and trepang, and who explain in the film the more recent difficulties facing the industry: seas were depleted in Indonesia, but trochus shells and shark fin were reportedly plentiful in Australian waters.

A spokesman for a Sama Bajo support group confirms that in earlier years nearby fish stocks were plentiful and life was easy; now, however, many of the nearby reefs have been overfished and destroyed, by the Sama Bajo people themselves as well as by fish-breeding areas of mangrove forests. The mangrove timber has been sold as firewood, the coral for building materials. Additionally, the Indonesian government have given fishing rights to Japanese and Taiwanese trawlers, so that much of the surrounding ocean is now overfished. Some Sama Bajo have relocated to the island of Rote, southwest of Kupang in West Timor. Newly settled or transient Sama Bajo fishing people now form a community near the town of Pepela (Papella) on Rote.

According to the film, some 3,000 fishermen were arrested by Australian authorities and 200 of their boats burned in the five years to 1993. Many of the fishermen arrested were already living below the poverty line, supporting families on Rote or back in Sulawesi. Often these fishermen chose imprisonment in lieu of paying a hefty fine, their incarceration paying off their fine at the rate of $25 per day – which meant leaving their families without support for these periods of time. The boats burned had an estimated value of $6,500 each, a very considerable amount of money in Indonesia in 1993.

Under a Memorandum of Understanding signed in 1974 between the Indonesian and Australian governments, traditional fishers have been allowed to fish in in Australian waters in an area below Ashmore Reef, known to Australian officials as 'the MOU Box'. But the agreement specifies they can only fish in 'traditional boats', which means sail-powered boats without auxiliary motors that might be used in emergencies, and without radios, which could keep them informed of changes in the weather, or summon help if trouble arose. In May 1991 five boats were destroyed in cyclonic weather (three disappearing entirely) resulting in the loss of a total of 60 men, leaving many widows and their children in Pepela. A total of 40 more Indonesian fishermen are estimated to have died in this area in the four years to 1993. These tragedies, little reported in Australia, were almost certainly inevitable given the ban placed on the use of potentially life-saving modern technology, in accordance with the letter of the law allowing only 'traditional' methods.

The film thus questions the rule of 'modern' Western law, which results in denying the right to apply modern technology to kinds of employment that have been traditional long before even the 'discovery' of Australia by Western explorers such as Dampier and Cook. It also highlights the consequences on the lives of actual people for whom the new Australian laws make little sense, to say nothing of the bureaucratic complexities of their formal arrest and imprisonment. The huge Australian Fishing Zone, based on the 200 nautical mile 'Exclusive Economic Zone' around Australia, introduced in November 1979, is an anomaly in this context: Ashmore Reef is about 120km south of Indonesia's Rote island where the fishermen are based, but

199 nautical miles from the Australian coastline. The film reports that in earlier times Rotinese people sometimes even grew corn on Ashmore Reef. Although not mentioned in the film, the Dutch never laid claim to the reef, but the British did, and it came to be regarded as an Australian external territory. In subsequent years the various Indonesian governments have not attempted to stake their claim to the reef, even though Indonesia did reciprocally assert a claim to a 200 nautical mile Indonesian Fishing Zone in March 1980. Despite the historical anomalies of all this, and the discrepancies and contradictions, the Australian law was ratified by the United Nations in the early 1980s.

As is manifest in his Bali films, *Below the Wind* shows John Darling's continuing interest in documenting how traditional communities in Indonesia live. Indeed, the film explores the interconnected lives of numerous communities in the region: not only the Sama Bajo in South East Sulawesi, but their new community in Rote; Aboriginal communities in Arnhem Land and north of Broome; Makassarese, who also historically had connections with Arnhem Land, and who have sometimes intermarried with Aboriginal people; Chinese Indonesian businessmen in Makassar; and Australian officials involved in arresting and incarcerating offenders. Despite the visual pleasure inherent in the romantic imagery of sea and sky, and sail-powered boats plying tropical waters, the film's sense of social detail, and the differences between the communities and of their outlooks on the situation are succinctly etched.

Most importantly, *Below the Wind* highlights the consequences of Australian law in ways that show how contingent and arbitrary it is, especially when applied to remote offshore waters, where there is little possibility of appeal. At the same time, the film recognises that some Aboriginal people, and Australian government officials, claim that the restrictions on the Sama Bajo fishermen are necessary on environmental grounds. One informant, for example, states that the methods used by Indonesians, increasingly desperate for a catch, are harmful to the environment by collecting trochuses that are still too young. But one Aboriginal woman, who in a cultural exchange visited the fishing communities at Pepela on Rote, says she now understands why the Sama Bajo people are at times predatory in their methods, saying they have no government-provided social security support to fall back on if the village economy fails.

The situation explored in *Below the Wind* is complex and varied, and both then and subsequently has been subject to rapid change. James J. Fox, in a detailed report published in 2002, states that throughout the 1990s the fisher people on Rote began to recognise that gathering trepang and trochus shells on the increasingly depleted Ashmore Reef was unviable. As a result, the emphasis had shifted almost exclusively to fishing for shark fin in the Timor Sea, using even newer methods of long-line fishing. While numerous boats were still being detained and burned, the well-connected and highly capitalised main boat owners on Rote (though not the poorer Sama Bajo) were able to recoup the loss of boats through the overall profits made, even though boats were burned quite frequently by the Australian authorities. However, under contractual arrangements it was the crews of all these boats who were liable for the loss of the confiscated fishing lines. The cost of replacing the lines is about half that of a boat, and hence they and the Sama Bajo were the main economic victims.[6]

For the rest of the 1990s, John planned several film projects, but his deteriorating health prevented any of them from coming to fruition. But extraordinary events in Bali a decade later provoked him into producing one more film.

The Healing of Bali (2003)

The *Healing of Bali* addresses the situation in Bali for the Balinese in the year after the bombing of the Sari Club and Paddy's Bar in Kuta Beach on 12 October 2002, in which 202 people were killed, 38 of them Indonesian, with similar numbers seriously injured. The first few minutes of the film uses actual footage of the horrendous fire that engulfed the clubs after the huge explosions, the subsequent carnage, and footage of victims in the various hospitals in South Bali; however, this moving and gentle film is primarily concerned with how surviving Balinese victims and relatives of the dead Balinese are coping after the event, and coming to terms with tragedy and loss.[7] Many of those interviewed are wives of Balinese or Javanese men killed in the blast. The first shot of the film shows a staircase of a temple, leading upwards, so that one sees only the blue sky and hears the tinkling of a temple bell. In this way the film at its very beginning suggests its predominantly spiritual and human concerns. Throughout, *The Healing of Bali* avoids sensationalism. Significantly it is the only one of John Darling's films that does not use a Western narrator. The voice-overs in the film are the different voices of those Balinese (and others) interviewed, with their remarks and comments being laid over film footage as it continues beyond the interviews.

A second major theme of the film, implicit at first, but becoming more explicit later on, is the lack of discrimination, indeed the underlying warmth, of the religiously tolerant Balinese people – including those most impacted by the events – towards local Muslim residents, in the face of the tragedy. The voice-over that gives an eyewitness account of the events of the night of 12 October, and to whom the film returns in intermittent interviews, is that of a Muslim Balinese traffic-control officer based in Kuta, Haji Bambang Priyanto, who within minutes of the explosion was involved in rescuing or caring for grievously injured victims and the dying. Throughout the whole night and late into the next morning he tended to their various needs – and was still anguished at the time the film was made. Subsequently Haji Bambang was a witness in the trial of the accused, relating the events that he witnessed.[8]

Later in the film, this presence of local Muslims in Bali, who themselves had also lost relatives, becomes a more explicit element of the film, with an interview with a young widow (and also her father-in-law) whose husband, a Muslim, died in the explosion. In the last scenes of the film, this young woman is seen talking at length on the seashore with a young Balinese Hindu woman who also lost her husband, showing the friendship between these two women.

One striking strand in the film is the concern of the Balinese with communicating with the dead, both an everyday aspect of their religion and part of their intimate experience in the weeks after the bombing. The reality of this, particularly for a non-Balinese audience, is most vivid in the reports of a young Australian woman – married to a Balinese who died in the Sari Club – who visited a *balian* (trance medium and healer) three days after the bombing, when her husband's remains had not yet been found. With her late husband speaking through the voice of the *balian*, she was informed of facts which at the time she herself and others did not know: first, that her husband's legs were still at the Sari Club and his upper torso and head were in the morgue at the Sanglah Public Hospital (facts confirmed six weeks later as a result of DNA testing of human remains); and second, that he had gone to the Sari Club not with Kadek (whom she believed to have accompanied him), but with Rudy, whom she did not even know at that stage was also still missing. The *balian* was able to give details such as Rudy's name, which she could only have known through the trance process.

This quite lengthy interview, relatively early in the film, is intercut with shots of a *balian* involved in trance communication with the deceased young daughter of another Balinese family, who died at the time the film was made.[9] The film therefore succeeds in giving a substantiating example of true information communicated, through a trance medium, from a subject who was dead – a common belief in Balinese daily life that had been mentioned in John's earlier works in regard to Balinese ancestor worship. Many Westerners might regard such beliefs as pure superstition, but the film substantiates communication with spirits of the dead by a direct participant of Australian origin. Neither the film nor the Australian widow attempts to explain the mysterious psychic and spiritual processes by which this transmission occurred.[10]

Other aspects of Balinese life in the aftermath of the tragedy are featured in the film. A Javanese Muslim woman, whose face was terribly burned in the fire, discusses the complications of wearing a therapeutic mask, and how the wearing of her mask over many months, while waiting for a further operation in Perth, impacts her young Balinese family. The film reports that the tragedy has resulted in numerous charitable organisations being set up, but that the large sums of money donated have rarely reached those impacted directly by the tragedy. Nevertheless, widows have banded together, and in one case an Australian man has donated sewing machines to a group of women, so that they can become self-supporting. A psychiatrist at the Bali International Medical Center hospital says that Balinese feel guilty because the bombings were a violation of the value they place on hospitality and the wellbeing of their guests. A group of widows, given permits to attend the trial of the accused, speak of how they were not able to remain in the presence of the terrorist Amrozi. Haji Bambang reports he could not look for long at Amrozi, even when told to do so by the presiding judge, for fear of being cursed by the sight of Amrozi's face. A young woman, one of the two surviving staff from the Sari Club, says that the club's wealthy owner, who lives in Germany, has never communicated with the victims of the tragedy, nor with the families of his numerous deceased staff. There is a quite lengthy sequence of a meeting of a *banjar* (local community organisation) attended only by male members, where the head of the *banjar* initiates a discussion about the contribution (four million rupiah, equal at the time to AUS$800) to be made by the families of each of the 20 victims associated with the *banjar*, to a group *ngaben* (cremation rituals), and whether the representatives of the families agree with the results of the deliberations by the *banjar*. After consulting together privately, representatives of the victims' families then announce that, although they agree in principle with the proposed arrangements for the *ngaben*, the *banjar* should consider giving subsidies to those poorer families who are unable to pay the agreed amount. The meeting of the *banjar* concludes with an affirmation by the *banjar* head that: 'Anything we do together will get the result we want. If you want money, we will get you money. If you want good feeling, you will get good feeling.'

Nevertheless, while widows in Bali are picking up the threads of their lives again, they will always miss their partners, even if their deceased partners are, as the Australian widow ruefully puts it about her Balinese husband, 'now in a better place'.

Conclusion

More than any formal training in filmmaking, it was John Darling's lengthy period of observation, participation and initiation into Balinese culture and society, as well as in other parts of Indonesia in the 1970s, that shaped his development as a filmmaker. He appears to have had natural talents, including an ability to quickly absorb possible modes of documentary presentation, and a discerning sense of what constituted significant material. He now had a unique and complex topic, about which he was quite passionate, and which needed documentation in film. John's films are objective in their stance (as seen in the comprehensive, indeed encyclopaedic *Bali Triptych*), but at the same time they provide access to Balinese subjectivity in a way that no other films have done, particularly in the engrossing *Lempad of Bali* and in his last film, *The Healing of Bali*. The detailed and poetic exposition of Balinese cultural issues that John achieved in *Lempad of Bali* and *Bali Triptych* ensured he had a basis for the ironic cross-cultural comparison so masterfully achieved in the lightweight but challenging and provocative *Bali Hash*.

His own underlying adventurous spirit coexists with his prescient concern for justice in the face of social contradictions and anomalies in Australia's relation to relatively impoverished Indonesians in *Below the Wind*, where he explores the lives and social background of the little known but intrepid Sama Bajo fishing people of Southeast Sulawesi and Rote island. The *Healing of Bali* not only addresses ways in which individual Balinese have engaged with the aftermath of the horrendous nightclub bombings in Bali in October 2002, but deepens one's sense – indeed confirms the presence – of uncanny spiritual forces at work in the island, something which, of all the filmmakers who have worked in Bali, it was for John to most fully achieve.

Notes

1. Cremation has been a central image in film and writing about Bali since the 1930s. In the process it has become a metaphor for the richness of collective meaning of Balinese culture. One effect of this has been the obscuring of the individual. Lempad was obviously an exceptional individual, but this film is one of the first studies, long before Unni Wikan's *Managing Turbulent Hearts* (1990) or Hildred Geertz's *Tales from a Charmed Life* (2005), to make visible the individual among the overwhelming collectivity of Balinese culture.
2. Darling refers in his journals to finding in film the expression he had previously sought, but was never satisfied with, in his poetry.
3. Jane Belo first went to Bali as the wife of the composer/musicologist Colin McPhee, but soon established her own place as an anthropologist. She published a series of short books on aspects of Balinese culture, culminating in a collection of essays by Western scholars resident in Bali at the time, called *Traditional Balinese Culture: Essays*. For a review of this collection see M. C. Ricklefs, *Bulletin of the School of Oriental and African Studies*, University of London, 34, no. 3, 1971, 679–680. (See also Jane Belo's bibliography in https://anthrosource.onlinelibrary.wiley.com/doi/pdfdirect/10.1525/aa.1968.70.6.02a00110). She also features prominently in James Boon's critical essay on that period (Boon 1976), as well as Tessel Pollman's even more critical one (Pollman 1990). In preparation for the Lempad film, John went through Belo's collected papers in the Library of Congress in New York and located dozens of fieldnotes with the label GM indicating their authorship by her assistant/secretary I Gusti Made Sumung.
4. The term originates with the Indian and Arab seafarers to refer to the islands at the far extent that the seasonal monsoon winds would allow them to sail to and return from. See also Reid (1988), p. 80.
5. Ironically, at the time of writing, this history is repeating itself – thirty years later.
6. Information on later developments within the Sama Bajo communities, and more recent concerns within this largely stalemated situation and its related considerations in international law, can also be found in a published work by the anthropologist Natasha Stacey (Stacey, 2007).
7. This film was at least partly motivated by the overwhelming emphasis in the Australian media on the Australian victims, and neglect of the Indonesia ones. This continues a theme throughout John's films of explaining to Australians their most immediate neighbour of which they know so little and understand even less.
8. Haji Bambang was in fact an old friend of John's, from his time in Kuta three decades earlier.

9   This séance involved people from the community John had lived in years earlier and had retained close contact with.
10 On this phenomenon see Linda Connor et. al. (1989).

References

Bateson, Gregory, 'Bali: The Value System of a Steady State', in Bateson, *Steps to an Ecology of Mind*, Chicago and London, University of Chicago Press, 2000, 107–127.

Bateson, Gregory and Mead, Margaret, *Balinese Character: A Photographic Analysis*, New York, New York Academy of Sciences, 1942.

Boon, J., 'The Birth of the Idea of Bali', *Indonesia* 1976, 22:71–84.

Connor, Linda, Asch, Patsy and Asch, Timothy, *Jero Tapakan; Balinese Healer: An Ethnographic Film Monograph*, Cambridge, Cambridge University Press, 1986.

Darling, John, *Lempad of Bali: A Memoir of a Master Artist and the Making of a Film*, eBook, 2014, formerly available from https://itunes.apple.com/us/book/lempad-of-bali/id835627146?mt=13 (accessed 19/01/2015).

Fox, James J. and Sen, Sevaly, 'A Study Of Socio-Economic Issues Facing Traditional Indonesian Fishers Who Access the MOU Box: A Report For Environment Australia', available from https://web.archive.org/web/20060827142957/http://rspas.anu.edu.au/people/personal/foxxj_rspas/Fishermen_MOU_BOX.pdf (accessed 19/01/2015).

Geertz, Hildred, 'How Lempad Changed the Course of Art in Bali' (book review), *Apollo Magazine*, 5 December 2015, available from http://www.apollo-magazine.com/review-lempad-of-bali/ (accessed 19/01/2015).

Mead, Margaret, and Macgregor, Frances Cooke, *Growth and Culture: A Photographic Study of Balinese Childhood*, New York, G.B. Putnam's Sons, 1951.

Pollman, T., 'Margaret Mead's Balinese: The Fitting Symbols of the American Dream', *Indonesia*, 1990, 49:1–36.

Reid, Anthony, *Southeast Asia in the Age of Commerce 1450–1680: Volume One, The Lands below the Winds*, New Haven, Yale University Press, 1988.

Said, Edward W., *Orientalism*, New York, Penguin Books, 1995.

Stacey, Natasha, *Boats to Burn: Bajo Fishing Activity in the Australian Fishing Zone* (Asia-Pacific Environment Monograph 2), Canberra, ANU Press, 2007.

Warren, Carol, *Adat and Dinas: Balinese Communities in the Indonesian State*, Oxford, Oxford University Press, 1993.

Lempad of Bali and the Translation of Aesthetics across Cultures

E. Douglas Lewis

As a research scholar in the then called Research School of Pacific Studies of the Australian National University, I came across a somewhat other-worldly fellow by the name of John Darling. He was busy with postproduction of a film about the life and death of Lempad, a Balinese artist and architect who, John told me, had lived 116 years. The following year, John released *Lempad of Bali*. In years that followed, our paths crossed a number of times in Canberra when he was in and out of the Australian National University working on various film projects. Living in different parts of Australia and on different islands in Indonesia when we were there, we remained acquaintances at a distance. As years threatened to turn into decades, I knew John through his post-Lempad films of Bali.

While I was engaged in the planning, production, and postproduction of a film about a rarely performed ritual in the domain of Wai Brama in east central Flores (Lewis, Asch, and Asch 1993), John's achievement with *Lempad* cemented itself in my mind. Our two films were very different, but then so were their subjects. Between 1987 and 2010 I screened *Lempad* every year in my undergraduate course on the anthropology of religion. As the screenings passed and writing about Wai Brama unfolded, I came to hold rather heterodox ideas about the nature of *culture* as a belabored and misused concept in anthropology. In time I realised that a central theme of John's film about the cremation of a Balinese artist was the relationship of a gifted and unusually prolific mind and its art to its social and historical environment. One of the attractions of John's film was that he and I both attributed creativity in the cultural and social realms firmly to individuals rather than some clanking metaphysical mechanism called culture.

I was concerned with how changes occur in an eastern Indonesian cosmology in adaptation to changes in its historical environment. John placed Lempad not at the centre of one particular substantial change in Balinese art, architecture, and aesthetics, but in a sustained continuity of effort through a long creative life that contributed substantially to a Bali very different from that into which he was born.

Gregory Bateson once proposed that grace is a necessary element in an artist's creativity. He then recorded Edmund Leach asking:

> 'How is it that the art of one culture can have meaning or validity for critics raised in a different culture? My answer would be that, if art is somehow expressive of something like grace or psychic integration, then the *success* of this expression might well be recognizable across cultural barriers. (Bateson 1972: 129)

Bateson's remark can be understood as saying that a work can manifest an aesthetic that transcends differences of culture (Lewis 2016: 142). Thus a work of art on its own can appeal to persons of different artistic backgrounds, but to be fully appreciated the context in which it is fully meaningful requires translation.

Here a film maker encounters a problem: people doing things (speaking is a doing) can be filmed. Culture is not phenomenal, but is noumenal, it is neither a material thing nor a force that makes anyone do anything. It cannot be filmed. If a film maker or writer wishes to establish 'cultural context' within which people act, then he must create the context in the idiom of his audience or readership rather than in the idiom of his subjects. At every turn, translation is required. John's solution to the challenge of translation was to film Lempad, the man, and to set him in the perceptible environment of his mortuary rites and the history of his island's people.

Darling and the Translation of Lempad's Bali

After having not seen him for some time, I bumped into Graeme MacRae in Ubud in 2016. I was staying with Rio Helmi, a longstanding friend who worked with John as a photographer during the filming of *Lempad*. That meeting precipitated two long conversations among the three of us, during which Helmi described Lempad as an *undagi*. In the languages of Bali and Java, an *undagi* is a carpenter; *ahli perundagian*, builder of traditional houses; in Bahasa Indonesia, expert.[1] Helmi commented that, in Bali, more than a carpenter:

> [an] *undagi* is a person who is not only an actual builder ... but is the person who knows how the proportions should be, how things should be adjusted; he knows the spiritual ... *Undagi* is a person who has an artistic [sensibility]. He knows how to bring things to life because he knows all the rules and the regulations, ... the distances ... and what they mean. (Rio Helmi in conversation with Graeme S. MacRae and E. Douglas Lewis. Recorded 12 June 2016.)

I Gusti Nyoman Lempad, the subject of John Darling's film, was, in other words, an *architect*. One of the *Oxford English Dictionary*'s definitions of *architect* reads: 'One who designs and frames any complex structure; *esp.* the Creator; one who arranges elementary materials on a comprehensive plan'. This accords with Darling's and Helmi's estimates of Lempad and it is this meaning I intend: the *undagi* as creator and cosmographer.

Translation is a much-underrated talent. George Steiner argued cogently that a translation of literature from its native language to another is a non-algorithmic (my word, not his) emprise. The result is not, nor should it aim to be, a tracing in another language over the original but an entirely new work itself. Thus, a work about an artist's life and work can itself be a work of art and can evince creativity and grace.

Lempad of Bali is about a death and a cremation ceremony in Bali. The cinematic images of the cremation, preparations for it, and its entailments, would need no explanation, no narrative, for an audience of Balinese. They would recognise instantly what they were seeing and understand the words of speakers in the film.[2] Thus, Darling's task was one of translation, to render images of people doing and saying unfamiliar things for not immediately fathomable reasons but meaningful to people of another place, time, and language. Thus, *Lempad* is an ethnographic film.

The cremation of Lempad's body, filmed by Blair and Darling in 1978, is the thread that sews the fabric of *Lempad of Bali* together. The cinematography takes us from the washing and shrouding of Lempad's corpse, to the purification rites that are part of the preparations, the preparation of offerings, the construction of the funeral tower, and the bamboo, timber, and cloth bull in which Lempad's body was burned, the cremation, to the scattering of his ashes in the surf at Sanur. The film reproduces well the increasingly intense sociality of Lempad's community as preparations unfold, which expands to include people from a wide region in Bali and camera toting-tourists appearing rather lost in the mêlée of the cremation's climax.

In one respect the film is a how to do it or (as Timothy Asch called the type) a process film, the process being that of a Balinese cremation. The film is also an oral narrative, a story in prose which becomes unmistakable when one transcribes and reads a transcript of the film's voice-over narration. While it is spoken by the actor Robin Ramsay in the film, the narration is Darling's and Blair's composition. Some passages sound a poetic meter and scansion, a division into metrical feet, a climbing up. The story begins with an ending, Lempad's death, in which the emic (the perspective of the Balinese participants) and etic (the point of view of the filmmaking guests) are clear and clearly set out Darling's field of translation. The living Lempad appears in the film, speaking, but his words are not translated for the viewer. In these appearances he is already removed, in good *Austronesian* fashion, as a sacred being himself, an almost ancestor, present but silent, his voice delegated to I Gusti Madé Sumung, his son, and from Sumung to the film makers.

Darling himself wrote that after filming Lempad's cremation rites, he and Blair realised that they could not make a film solely from that footage:

> ... while we were filming these activities, it became apparent to us that in making a film about such a man as Lempad, it was not enough to purely record the Balinese ritual of death which, after all, are pretty much the same for any of the higher castes of Bali. ... We decided to add two further themes into the structure of the cremation rites ... The idea developed that we should attempt to show Lempad's unique life through his art and the changing times of Bali over the last hundred years in a manner similar to Balinese genealogical histories, called *babad*, which do their part

in reinforcing the identity of the present generation by making them proud of their ancestors. (Darling 2016: 17)

Achieving their aim, Darling knew, would require substantial extra-frame information and translation.

Two translations were required. First, the translation or glossing of speech in Balinese and Bahasa Indonesia on film. Second, the translation of the concepts, social relationships, and praxes of the Balinese, and the cosmology and religion articulated by the mortuary rites seen on film. In other words, a translation of the culture in which Lempad lived and whose work transformed the art of a people embedded in a complex social, cultural, and historical universe of extraordinary vitality and beauty.

Given differences in language and culture between the Balinese on film and Darling's Anglophone audience, he needed a window through which to communicate extra-frame information to explain the images he put before his audience. To do that, he needed first to alert his audience to the need for such a window. Darling provides the necessary window through which his communication with his audience is not about Bali, Lempad or the cremation, but about differences of language and culture and about the filmmakers' intentions. At the outset, he establishes that, while it is about Lempad, the narration is first a translation of language and culture from Lempad's to that of Darling's audience. The metamessage informs the anglophone audience that the voice speaking English is not that of Lempad or his son or any other Balinese, but the voice of a translator. Indeed, the metamessage assures the audience that the film's Balinese characters cannot communicate with their audience without a translator.

Twenty-two minutes and twenty four seconds into the film, Darling emphasises this point. We see people carving wood sculptures for the cremation. Darling tells us, through the voice of the narrator, 'Almost the entire village community turns out every day to assist in the work' (22.24). '... There is a feeling that Lempad's spirit is controlling his own cremation. His final work of art on this earth'(22.40).[3]

Images of preparation for the cremation continue, but with the sudden, intrusive noise of a television with screechy, poor quality sound (22.48). Five seconds later (22.53), the film cuts to footage of a black and white television screen showing an image of a house exploding. The voice-over tells us: 'Television is a very recent introduction to Bali. It entered Lempad's house only two months before his death. For most Balinese this is the first glimpse of the world the tourists come from. The western invasion is complete' (22.54).

This is an abrupt and anomalous leap from the activities of people calmly preparing for the cremation. Why this joltingly disruptive intrusion of a western TV program and its noisomely violent images? Darling uses the television receiver to remind his audience that he himself, a filmmaker who has lived in Bali many years, is nonetheless a westerner and, in the film, the creator of context.

At 23.15 we return to colour footage of a woman watching television while plaiting a palm-leaf offering. One second later the film cuts suddenly to an odd musical soundtrack with a black and white photograph of a steamship supporting the Dutch invasion of Bali: Ramsay's voice skilfully changes pitch and tempo. The narration over additional archival images of the Dutch military operation with a soundtrack of marching feet and explosions of artillery shells reads:

> It began back on September the sixth nineteen hundred and six when Lempad was in his forty-fourth year. A Dutch fleet stood off the beach at Sanur, which these days is densely covered with tourist hotels. After their early failures to subdue the island, the

Dutch were taking no chances. They put ashore three battalions of infantry, cavalry and machine gun units and two batteries of field artillery. They met fierce but inadequate resistance.

Over archival photographs, narration describes the subsequent massacre of the prince of Badung and his followers. The segment ends with the narrator saying: 'It was to take two years and four more such incidents before Bali was brought fully under Dutch control.'

With the sudden shift from ethnographic footage of women plaiting palm leaves while watching a newly installed television receiver, to the stark historical images and sounds of a military operation, Darling announces to his audience that what follows is the meta-information needed to expand the context of Lempad's cremation. It is dramatically and brilliantly done, with a poet's shift from a calm and reflective Balinese timbre and mood to a harsh, urgent, and jarring western idiom.

Nowhere do we learn explicitly Darling's qualifications for providing guidance. Rather, as the film unfolds, Darling's cinematic voice is absorbed by the montage and becomes a character among his subjects. The craft of the narration suffices to establish Darling's words as credible narrative.

The narration of an ethnographic film requires the translation, or at least the glossing, of words spoken on camera by the film's subjects. The techniques employed by ethnographic filmmakers in the era of *Lempad* included voice-over narrations laid down in post-production. This technique can work well but it requires muting the original recordings of subjects speaking on camera and the consequent loss of linguistic information. Another technique is the provision of translations of speech on camera in subtitles. Subtitling is constrained by technical limitations. No number of words in a subtitle can capture and translate completely all that is said in film of complex verbal interactions. So, too, subtitling entails a loss of information, both because of the impossibility of a subtitled literary text tracking completely the evolution of speech on film and also because the viewer's eyes must flicker between unfolding cinematic images and the intrusive subtitles.[4]

Darling employed a technique that was falling out of favour in some quarters of ethnographic filmmaking by the end of the 1970s. He chose a didactic, that is, explanatory, voice-over narration in English to provide his audiences with the information they needed to understand not merely the evanescent filmic images of the moment, but something of the depth and subtleties of meaning known implicitly by Balinese themselves.

The result was, in my opinion, one of the most sensitive and effective didactic narrations in the repertoire of ethnographic films that I know. Moreover, the transcription of his narrative reads very well as prose literature when extracted from the film.[5] The writing is simple, direct, sparse, and unambiguous. It is designed to be spoken but it is a delight to read. It is the prose one might expect of a poet whose spoken words and intonations move beautifully with the risings and fallings, the stretchings and compressions, of the images and montage of the film. The reading is Ramsay's, but the script and the plan are Darling's, a literary *undagi*'s.

Darling's narration, more than the archival images we see, anchors Lempad in his place and time. The narration over Lempad's drawing of Rare Angon and the Birth of Kala is a very good example of Darling's talent for providing extra-frame information (see image no. 10):

> His paintings and drawings developed a new and refined style. Here the great god Shiva tricks his wife by sending her to earth to get milk from a virgin cow. Disguising himself as a handsome

cowherd, Shiva offers to provide it for her if she will mate with him. Determined to fulfil her task, she agrees but, suddenly distressed by her unfaithfulness, she pulls free and Shiva's sperm falls to the ground, from which grows the demonic and destructive Bhatara Kala. The three-petalled symbol on one fang indicates his semi-divine status. The western visitor on the other is Lempad's ironical addition to the legend. Bhatara Kala is the god of catastrophe. (38.20)

The film ends as quietly as it began, suggesting that despite the turmoil of the previous 116 years, the culture of the people of Bali abides.

The film is narrated throughout by Robin Ramsay, who is reading John Darling's text. No speech, neither in the Balinese language nor in Indonesian, is subtitled in English translation. Sumung's expository comments on his father's life and work are not in Balinese but in Bahasa Indonesia and are spoken in conversation with Darling (presumably). Where Sumung speaks on camera,[6] the film editor fades his Indonesian and cues in the voice of B. Joseph (identified in the end credits as 'Voice Over'), speaking an English translation of Sumung's Indonesian.

Voice-over narration of non-fiction films is always beset by problems. A viewer wonders, whose voice is this I am listening to? What's the narrator's qualification for telling me about the images I am seeing? Problems of narration are far greater in anthropological documentaries and ethnographic films than in documentaries whose subjects speak the audience's language. When films are about subjects of one linguistic and social group intended for viewing by audiences of another, the difficulties magnify. If a narrator is telling his audience what subjects on film are saying in a language the viewer cannot understand, a first question is, 'how does this guy (the narrator) know what the people in the film are saying?' How does he happen to know anything at all about the language, culture, social relationships, and social practices of the people depicted in the film? The filmmaker needs to establish their knowledge and authority without making the film intrusively *about* the film's makers.

There are many technical and aesthetic challenges in creating in a voice-over narration the translation of the complex social relations and cosmology lurking on the Balinese side of the cultural and linguistic boundaries between them and the audience. Narrations come in identifiable types.

There are didactic, explanatory, or interpretive narrations, in which a narrator lectures on the subject of the film or explains what is happening on film and why as the moving images progress. A narration may explain what a subject is doing on film by interpreting the subject's actions or by proposing motivations for the subject's actions or hypothesising what a subject was thinking – always an impossible aim – when doing what he was doing on film.

There are complementary narrations, those that provide a viewer with information additional to that in the cinematic images by contextualising people's actions on film and situating them in their social and ideational milieux in such a way that encourages the viewer to devise an explanation for the film's images and sounds.

An effective film narration may use both of these forms of narrative while avoiding redundancies of information already in the images themselves. John Darling's aim was explanation by the contextualisation of Lempad's life and work. Here, the filmmaker is freest to develop the narrative that best addresses what he thinks will be his audiences' questions about the images, the events they record, what people and participants in those events are doing and saying, and why they are doing them. Darling was aware that words, whether those of a narrator, a black and white title interposed between a film's shots, or subtitled or voiced-over translations of the utterances of subjects speaking on film can complement a film's images and native sound in such a way as to expand greatly the film's meaning and impact. Nevertheless, he takes care to limit his extra-frame information. A film can be strangled by over-contextualisation.

Complementary narrations convey that the filmmaker and his subjects are engaged in a collaboration to explore a theme, a topic, an event, a situation, arising in or from the subjects' world. The filmmaker does not intrude into the subject of the film more than is minimally required. Yet while the presence of the filmmaker is evident, it is unobtrusive and indeed unseen.

I have spoken to viewers who asked about the lack of subtitled translations of on-camera speech in *Lempad*. These were at coordinated screenings in a teaching semester that included *A Celebration of Origins* and the films about Bali from the Aschs' collaboration with Linda Connor. The Asch films and *Lempad* were made at about the same time; indeed the filmmakers knew each other and each others' work, and were occasional colleagues in Canberra. Both *Lempad* and *Celebration* are about large-scale rituals in Indonesia and both focus on one or a few individuals who guide viewers through their communities. Among his options, Darling chose voice-over translations of speech rather than subtitled translations. This may have been because the only long and complex utterances we see in *Lempad* were those of a second narrator, Lempad's son, Sumung, who is credited (54.35) with conceiving the film. Enough of Sumung's remarks can be heard to determine that he was speaking Bahasa Indonesia on camera rather than Balinese. At 11.52, we hear Sumung begin a sentence in Bahasa Indonesia – 'Enam bulan, sebelum meninggal, dia sudah memikirkan dia akan meninggal, sering di puri kita dengar...', 'six months before [he] died, he was already thinking his death was near, we often heard this at the temple ...'[7] – before the synchronous sound fades and the voice-over translation is cued in. These voice-overs occur only four times in the film. Darling may have thought that the appearance of subtitles in the film would be distracting, and so provided voice-overs. I think another impulse was at work.

Darling tells a complex story of interwoven themes, of Lempad, his family and community life, his work, and Balinese history and society. Stories are told by voice. Sumung's contributions to the telling of the story were spoken, and so their words are translated and heard in English in the film. Darling's story is of Balinese society, history and art, told through the life of a gifted man, with that man's relation to that society and his transformation of art an important part of it. If we accept the OED's definition that, between genius and talent, genius is regarded as 'the higher of the two, as "creative" and "original"', then Darling's treatment of I Gusti Nyoman Lempad's works convinces us that they are of genius.

Teaching Anthropology with *Lempad of Bali*

A film is ethnographic if it portrays the lives and activities of a people of one language and society for viewing by, and in the language of, people of another. An ethnographic film can be referred to as an anthropological film if it addresses a topic or theory in anthropology. Such a film must reach beyond its images of effervescent scenes of community life to address questions about human nature more broadly. It need not do this explicitly if it raises in the minds of its audience questions about the nature of human sociality and the human mind and points toward answers, however debatable they may be.

I found *Lempad* to be an excellent film for teaching anthropology. It fulfils the requirements of depicting life in places and among people quite different from those of my students (except when I teach in Indonesia) and it motivates thinking about topics and questions of fundamental anthropological interest. Foremost of these, to my mind, is creativity in culture and the relationship and responsibility of creative individuals to their community. The unstated theme of individual creativity in relation to culture makes teaching with *Lempad* rewarding.

Social anthropology is not usually about individuals. It is about the constitution of community by its elemental social groups. Nevertheless, anthropologists learn what they know from individual members of the societies they study and their cultures (that pesky c- word). While anthropologists may think of culture as reified by groups in their members' social activities, it is a construct of the mind located in the central nervous systems of individual human beings, in whose minds it subsists. What we anthropologists are after is the 'culture' which is carried in the minds of associated persons. But no human being has direct access to other minds. We can only learn what they choose to reveal through their speech, the things they do and make, their quotidian activities and their interactions with others. We then assume that these reflect, express, are functions of, or signal and symbolise what goes on in their heads. This assumption has never been tested, proven or disproven in anthropology.

Lempad spent his life creating balance (Bahasa Indonesia *keseimbangan*) during, Darling tells us, the most traumatic century in Bali's history: successive invasions of the Dutch pacification, the eruptions of the volcanic Mount Agung, the Japanese occupation during the Second World War, a war for independence, absorption into the

Republic of Indonesia, and acculturative encounters with hordes of visitors from overseas. While he documents the social and historical turbulence of Lempad's time, Darling is careful to impute no causality between those historical events and Lempad's work – except that, at one point, he notes that during the Japanese Occupation Lempad withdrew into himself:

> During ten years of chaos, Lempad had retreated into a meditative, almost catatonic state and produced no works of art. He was later to explain that the disarray of the world obliged him to turn inwards in search of personal serenity. (35.20.)
>
> Friends and family were convinced that he would soon die. They little realized that, approaching the age of ninety, he was about to embark on an artistic renaissance. (35.42.)

No causation, but an understandable reaction of a mind driven by an impulse to create orderly art amid chaos in the world around him.

The film teaches us that at the heart of all innovation and change in culture there are individual, creative persons, the instigators of change. They may be common or scarce, depending upon time and place. They may be doers or thinkers, but they have been our pathfinders since our ancestral generations on the Pleistocene savannahs of Africa. The underlying theme of creativity can generate questions, discussion, and thought among young students of our species. If our main responsibility as teachers is to convey what we have learned of the world to the young people temporarily in our care, with *Lempad of Bali*, John Darling has given teachers of anthropology and Asian societies an exquisitely wrought tool for that task.

A Final Remark

> For the attainment of grace, the reasons of the heart must be integrated with the reasons of the reason. (Gregory Bateson, perhaps recalling Blaise Pascal's *Pensées*; §§ 183, 185, 277, 282 *et alibi*)

No translation is ever precise, much less true. Translation is not algorithmic; the adjective does not apply. Words in languages carry histories, polysemies, proprieties, nuances. The sentences they make up, governed by syntaxes and pragmatics unique to each, comprise radically different worlds of expression. Translation from one language to another is difficult and requires a translator who knows well both two languages and two worlds, and who possesses acutely fine judgment.

The phrase *true translation* is an oxymoron; it cannot be expected of any transduction of language or imagery. We translate when we attempt a crossing from one universe of thought and language, syntax and symbolism, to another. A translation necessarily requires a recreation, a work that is not the original transported mechanically from one universe to another, but is *sui generis* a new work. Thus translation, both reproductive and innovatory (Steiner 1975:26), carries its own poiesis. At its finest, it requires a sensitivity to language, from the pen of a master, and is itself a creation. John Darling, the poet, possessed this sensitivity and accomplished a cogent translation from the genius of Lempad, his works, and his Bali into cinematography and the concepts and idiom of English, a singular achievement.

Why so much time, effort and artifice devoted, in the film's final words, to the disposal of Lempad's mortal remains? If a story is an answer to a question, this one is well answered in the film. In John Darling's *Lempad of Bali* we glimpse the grace that marked the life in art of an extraordinary human being and that inspired a gifted film maker.

Notes

1. For an excellent account of the sociology of Balinese architectural knowledge and the status of *undagi* in Balinese society see MacRae and Parker (2002).
2. A comparison of the English version of *Lempad* and the version in Bahasa Indonesia (Darling 1980) makes this plain: I Gusti Madé Sumung's on camera speech in Bahasa Indonesia requires no voice-over translation for an Indonesian audience and thus does not carry the voice over translation of the English version.
3. Time stamps refer to the Ronin Films DVD release of the English version of *Lempad of Bali* (Darling 1980).
4. I have written about the technical difficulties of subtitling. See E. Douglas Lewis, Timothy Asch, & Patsy Asch, 1994, *A Celebration of Origins*, 16 mm film, Watertown, MA. The challenge of narrations in *Lempad* is quite clear when comparing the English language and Indonesian versions of the film.
5. Some, but not all, of Darling's text is available (Darling 2014, 2016). I transcribed the narration directly from the film and, when I compared the transcript to the published version, I found differences between the published text and the version spoken by Robin Ramsay in the film. I would be interested to know if the film version arose from modifications from Darling's original text during the recording of Ramsay or from editorial changes by Darling when he prepared the text for publication.
6. At 5:40-6:10, 8:36-8:59, 17:13-17:48, and 28:48-29:55 in both the English and Bahasa Indonesia versions of the film.
7. There is a minor anomaly here: *puri* means palace, whereas a temple is a *pura*. In the context either could be correct, but either way there is no essential loss of meaning.

References

Bateson, Gregory, 'Style, Grace, and Information in Primitive Art', in *Steps to an Ecology of Mind: Collected Essays in Anthropology, Psychiatry, Evolution, and Epistemology*, San Francisco, Chandler Publishing Company, 1972.

Carpenter, Bruce W. *et al*, *Lempad of Bali: The Illuminating Line*, Ubud, Museum Puri Lukisan, 2016.

Darling, John, *Lempad of Bali*, Canberra, Ronin Films, 1980.

Darling, John, *Lempad of Bali: A Memoir of a Master Artist and the Making of a Film*, Jakarta, Equinox Publishing, 2014.

Darling, John, *Lempad of Bali: A Memoir of a Master Artist and the Making of a Film*, Taman Sari Productions Pty. Ltd, 2016, http://lempad.com/.

Lewis, E.D., 'Authenticity and the Textiles of Sikka: An Essay on the Apposition of Values', in Julian C.H. Lee and Marco Ferrarese (eds.), *Punks, Monks and Politics: Authenticity in Thailand, Indonesia and Malaysia*, London, Rowman & Littlefield, 2016.

Lewis, E. Douglas, Asch, Timothy and Asch, Patsy, *A Celebration of Origins*, 16 mm film, Watertown, Massachusetts, DER, 1993.
MacRae, Graeme and Parker, Samuel, 'Would the Real *Undagi* Please Stand Up? On the Social Location of Balinese Architectural Knowledge', *Bijdragen tot de Taal-, Land- en Volkenkunde* 158 (2), 2002: 253–281.
Pascal, Blaise, *Pensées*. Grand Rapids, Michigan, Christian Classics Ethereal Library, 2010, formerly available from http://www.ccel.org/pascal/pensees.html.
Steiner, George, *After Babel*. London, Oxford University Press, 1975.

Making *The Healing of Bali*

Sara Darling with Thomas Reuter

A note from Graeme MacRae

The Healing of Bali *was John's last film, made in response to the shocking bombing in the heart of the crowded tourism precinct of Kuta in 2002. In spite of his debilitating health problems, John felt compelled to help by telling the story in a way that he knew few others would be able to. Fortunately, he had Sara to manage his health and household as well as the production side of the film. They rented a large house in Krobokan, not far from Kuta, and employed members of John's old neighbourhood (Taman) in Ubud as cooks, drivers, equipment wranglers and security guards. They obtained some funding from SBS Television and the Research School of Pacific and Asian Studies at ANU, which at the time was headed by Professor James Fox, an old friend of John's.*[1]

Nevertheless, the budget was tight (as always) and they had to work fast amid rapidly unfolding events in Bali. John mobilised his old networks of contacts in Bali and called in favours from friends such as Rio Helmi and Bruce Carpenter. The mainstream media was saturated with coverage of the bombing itself, the (mostly Australian) victims, and the hunt, capture and subsequent trial of the perpetrators. The film touches on these, but they are only the background to the key people in the story, including Haji Bambang, a Muslim hero in the immediate aftermath. The focus of The Healing of Bali *is, as the title suggests, the ways in which local people and communities recovered from and made sense of the tragedy – both in material* (sekala) *and metaphysical* (niskala) *terms. At the heart of the film are the interwoven stories of three women whose husbands died in the tragedy: one Balinese Hindu, one (Javanese) Muslim, and one Australian married to a Balinese.*

For Balinese, the complex and expensive process of cremation is essential for the after-life of the deceased and considerable attention was given to the challenges involved in these circumstances. Because parts of these women's husbands' remains were never found, they consulted a balian *('paranormal' is the translation used in the film) for direct information and advice from the deceased. These consultations and other scenes of ritual are illustrated indirectly by filming a real trance séance and temple ceremonies involving people from Taman. Another sub-theme is the contributions of various people in and from Australia providing medical, financial and employment assistance. While there are moments of regret, such as the money raised and not spent on the victims, the overriding theme of the film is the physical and emotional healing and especially of renewed bonds between Balinese Hindus and their Muslim neighbours.*

Like all of John's films, The Healing of Bali *is sensitive to its subjects, deeply moving and informed by and infused with his deep knowledge of Bali and her people. In this case, however, there is no voice-over narration – the subjects all speak for themselves, in their own languages, through subtitles. It was, like most of his other films, designed for screening on Australian television, in a standard one-hour slot. It premiered on SBS Television a year later, on the first commemoration of the bombing. Here, Sara (with help from Thomas Reuter) takes us behind the scenes.*

Making *The Healing of Bali*

For many Australians, the night of Saturday, 12 October 2002 can be compared with 11 September 2001. People recall exactly what they were doing when they heard the unbelievable news that two bombs had exploded in the popular nightclub district of Kuta Beach in Bali.

John, who was already chronically ill, constantly monitored the world news. On that day, he thus heard the first report on radio at 3:26am. The first report was 'Breaking News: 3 Dead in Bali Explosion' and added that at least five others were injured. However, by 5am we sat dumbstruck watching live TV coverage from the Kuta bombsite and Sanglah Hospital, as the full scale of the disaster unfolded.

> The number of Australians killed was unknown last night, but it was likely the attack would cause the greatest single loss of Australian lives overseas during peace-time. (*The Canberra Times*, 14 October 2002)

Three weeks later, John and I were less than 500 meters from the car bomb site on Jalan Legian, where I bargained for a bum-bag to carry camera-lens covers and tripod connections to film the documentary John was directing and we were producing together.

For much of the next year, we lived and filmed in Bali to ensure *The Healing of Bali* would be ready for screening on SBS TV a year later, on 12 October 2003, to commemorate the anniversary of the Bali bombings.

Whether to make the film or not came down to a giant leap of faith. Within a few days of the bombings, John had already heard there was to be a large ceremony called *Taur Agung*. In Balinese, this literally means 'great payment' or 'sacrifice', and it is performed only after major disruptive events. The last one had been held over twenty years before.

Using this information before it was generally known, John phoned and emailed many of the television channels, using his connections from the eight internationally screened documentaries he had already directed and produced. His idea was to use the *Taur Agung* as the centrepiece of a documentary or even a short current affairs item, or to provide consultant services to an in-house film crew.

All attempts to obtain funding were met with bureaucratic obstruction. Deadlines for periodic film-funding schemes were months away, and so we were at an impasse, as the date for the ceremony in Bali had already been determined.

We realised that we needed to clarify our reasons for making a film on such a subject. First, John believed that this ancient culture had a different way of grieving that may offer insights and strength to Australians. Second, he decided that his health had improved to the point where he felt that, with assistance, he could direct a film. Finally, there is a belief in Hinduism called *dharma*, which has many meanings including fulfilling one's personal duty. John felt this film was a way in which he could repay Bali for all that it had given him. He felt dismay that Indonesian victims of the bombings had not received much media attention or material aid, that the number of local victims was not clear, and that something needed to be done to rectify this. The film's title emerged from these strong beliefs. John wanted to show how the local Balinese community in Kuta (and throughout Bali) came together to heal itself through its religious beliefs and rituals.

The die was cast. We had started gathering research for a documentary film from day one, so we were already in pre-production mode. My background in nursing, education, film and research meant that John and I worked well as a team. Our son Toby was our production assistant, and later this role was undertaken by our daughter Danielle.

Having committed to filming the *Taur Agung*, the Research School of Pacific and Asian Studies at ANU in Canberra, where John was a Visiting Fellow, offered us a small loan. This was enough to film this important ceremony. In addition, Garuda Airlines offered us a number of free return plane tickets.

We worked frantically for the final three days to be ready to fly out from Sydney. Packing items included culturally appropriate clothes for different temple ceremonies, as each cloth has different meanings. I became aware we were working in many areas with intense pressure to achieve goals in a short space of time. We decided in one of our brief moments of reflection that we were probably each doing the work of three people. We pressed on with two hours' sleep each night, realising we had only one chance to film this ceremony.

After another sleep-deprived night, we drove to Sydney from Canberra to catch our early morning flight. After a trouble-free three-hour drive, we ground to a halt in Sydney's heavy morning traffic for almost an hour. We arrived at the airport in a panic. But Garuda management not only knew we were coming, they had set aside twelve huge plastic bags of clothes donated for victims of the bombings.

As Sydney slid away beneath us, I took a moment to look around the cabin and realised that there were very few people on the flight. No wonder they had waited for us!

As we approached Bali, fishing boats were bobbing in the calm ocean. Along the western cliffs we could see large hotel developments interspersed with small temples dotted along the cliff tops. A Balinese Brahmana priest, or *pedanda*, told us some months later of the significance of these large tourist resorts. He said that when Bali was first settled, the Gods told the people to build temples at particular locations along the coast. These are significant places commemorating the journey of Sang Hyang Nirartha, a legendary Hindu saint from Java, who is reported to have meditated at these locations on his pilgrimage around the island.

It was believed that these temples form a 'spiritual fence' around Bali to protect it from the evil of the outside world. With the rapid development of tourism along the coast and luxury hotel resorts and golf courses now jutting out across the cliffs, this 'fence' had apparently been broken. The *pedanda* lamented that this allowed terrorists to enter Bali.

Less than three weeks prior to the Bali bombings, we had attended a C.E.W. Bean Dinner in Canberra on 25 September 2002 to honour war correspondents. The guest speaker was the Minster for Defence, Robert Hill. Retrospectively, I cannot decide whether it was part of a deliberate strategy when critical information was delivered to a room full of journalists, late in the evening, after enjoying a three-course meal with plenty of alcohol flowing. The common thread of his speech, as it moved geographically from one country to another, was what Senator Hill referred to as 'tentacles of terror'.

On the drive home with a friend, I recall laughing about the alliteration he had used. I was not laughing two and a half weeks later when the bombs exploded in Bali. I realised then that Senator Hill was in fact talking about the spread of Al-Qaeda through allegedly affiliated Jemaah Islamiyah cells into Southeast Asia, and indeed Australia.

Australian intelligence apparently had been notified that 'soft targets' in Indonesia where Westerners gather had been selected as potential sites for terrorist attacks. The USA upgraded its warning for travellers visiting Bali a few days before the bombs exploded, but Australia did not.

In Denpasar, we passed through Immigration and Customs in record time, as there were so few people in the airport. Outside there was an almost complete absence of tourists. Footpaths that were usually packed with visitors were empty.

The roads at Kuta beach are usually swarming with tourists on motorbikes and in taxis. We did not see either. In fact, we saw only three foreigners on our drive to the hotel. Normally, we would have seen hundreds on the sidewalks and hundreds more on the beaches. For an economy that was based on tourism, we could see that financial devastation was looming.

The next morning, we ate at a restaurant that was a traditional place for Australians to congregate. The Legian Garden Restaurant had a full range of Australian Football League jumpers displayed on the wall above the bar. The restaurant had cable TV which continually screened Australian sport.

As we walked in, we realised we were the only customers. This was a novel experience for us, but it was to become the normal situation in most restaurants over the coming months. Our son pointed to the coaster mats taped under the glass tabletops. The messages written on them were a real shock. There were hand-written notes asking if anyone had seen these people alive, and listing contact details. Even more chilling was our awareness that some of those people whose names were written on coaster mats had been killed.

Next, we needed to access the bombsite, which proved challenging. We had not realised the immense scale of the area that had been affected. Jalan Legian is the major road running from Kuta through Legian, and the bomb site was located in the centre of that road.

After walking past rows of shops with shattered windows, we suddenly entered an open space with overwhelming evidence of devastation everywhere. Electricity poles and transmitters were twisted into macabre angles, surrounding buildings were partly razed to the ground, and the Sari Club site was flattened entirely. What was left of Paddy's Bar was a mere shell of the famous gathering place, with some sections of outside walls remaining, and inside a blackened spiral staircase and the remains of the bar. Charred bar stools and broken glass littered the floor.

Blackened car shells, distorted and twisted, had all been pushed together to create a tangled line of windowless shells. Yet even on these mangled objects the Balinese had placed beautiful offerings. One of the characters in the film, Warti, tells of her young husband who was a Haagen Daas delivery driver and was decapitated by the bomb blast.

Once I registered my surroundings, I became aware of the silence, broken only by the whirring noise of small bamboo windmills handmade by the Balinese, so that the noise would call attention to the fact that the Gods were needed at that location.

I came to understand this Balinese logic further when we interviewed a *pedanda* priest who was to conduct a ceremony at the Kuta Beach location, two days before the *Pamarisuddha Karipubhaya*, the Great Purification Ceremony. He told John that where the bomb exploded at Jalan Legian was where three roads intersected, and in Balinese cosmology this is a place of souls who had lost their way. Originally, there had been a children's graveyard located at this three-way intersection, which also signals spiritual danger in Balinese cosmology.

Prior to leaving Canberra, John had located a newspaper article describing a Javanese Muslim man, who on the night of the bombings had directed many of the rescues of injured people. He had worked tirelessly throughout the night and was known as the 'Muslim hero', but no one knew his name or followed up to report further on this brave man.

During one of our film shoots at the bombsite before the Great Purification ceremony, our son spotted an Indonesian man wearing an Australian Federal Police cap. Toby approached the man in the cap, who told him that he had been at the site on the night of 12 October. He was reluctant to be interviewed, but eventually agreed.

Toby took John over to the man and as Toby started to introduce him, the man in the cap said 'John?' I have a photo of that moment of recognition, as he realised that this was the same John who had played chess with him on the beach as an 8-year-old. He had beaten my husband soundly and repeatedly, and as a result John never played chess again! His name? None other than Haji (the title of a Muslim who has made the pilgrimage to Mekkah). Agus Bambang, whose family had moved to Bali from Java some 70 years ago.

His father Pranoto had been a good friend of John's in the early 1970s. He was a Sufi Muslim, an adherent of a gentle mystical version of Islam, and he was also an amazing musician, playing both the flute and sitar. He established the first juice bar on Kuta Beach and was involved in hotel management and tourism when the industry was just beginning in Bali. He cared for all Westerners who visited Bali. He was the person to see when you first arrived in Kuta for accommodation, information and support. A kind and wonderful man, he refused to be paid for his work.

We agreed to interview Bambang in the remains of what once was a shop, next to the Sari Club site. We stood between the two remaining crumbling walls, with no roof and rubble underfoot. Toby held back metal rods that created shadows across Bambang's face and the interview began. At one point I looked down and saw we were standing amongst the remains of bloodstained clothes. Despite the sweltering heat in the middle of the day, Bambang's interview was full of passion, emotion and energy. Afterwards, John told us we had indeed found the Muslim hero mentioned in the Australian news. It was only that evening we realised that Bambang was also fasting for Ramadan.

During the interview, with tears in his eyes, he explained proudly: 'My father Pranoto taught me about humanity, I was taught about morality and values, and this is me, Bambang, the son of Pranoto.' He continued, 'I never see people as white-skinned, black-skinned, Catholic, Christian, Muslim, Buddhist or Hindu. I see them all as humans that God invented to be here.'

Prior to leaving Australia, John realised that, as he had been too unwell to visit Bali for more than five years, he needed an academic with expertise in Balinese culture who was well informed of recent changes in Bali. Indonesianists at ANU recommended Dr Thomas Reuter, an anthropologist from the University of Melbourne's Asia Institute for this task. Fortunately, Thomas was available to travel and we forged an invaluable relationship. Thomas's extensive knowledge and insights provided additional layers that enriched the foundation of cultural knowledge which underpinned this film.

One of the film shoots that Thomas accompanied us on was to the neighbourhood where one of the bombers, Amrozi, had lived while in Bali. We also visited the office of the Majelis Ulama Indonesia (MUI), the primary state-sponsored Muslim organisation in Indonesia, a few doors down from Amrozi's residence. Its head denied all knowledge of Amrozi's plans, though he conceded that he had met him. Apparently, Amrozi had kept to himself and not engaged much with the community. The head of MUI strongly disapproved of the bombing but, at the same time, we found that his organisation was on a mission to Islamise Bali. A graph on the wall of this office showed the rising number of Muslims as a proportion of the population of Bali as a whole, predicting when Muslims are likely to become the majority on an island, frequented by millions of foreigners hoping to experience not just its beaches but its iconic Hindu temples, arts and religious events. Balinese view these developments and the aspirations of Muslim organisations with rising concern. This makes it all the more remarkable that there were no reprisals against the Muslim minority on the island in the aftermath of the bombings.

In Balinese culture it is considered inappropriate to display anger. So how, after an incident as devastating as these bombings, did Balinese people express their feelings? We met a psychiatrist, Dr Denny Thong, at a meeting for survivors. I noticed that many of them looked dazed and had cotton wool in their ears, as a result of damage to their eardrums from the bombs. It was a very hot, sultry day, and food, water and blankets were being distributed to the survivors.

Dr Thong told us that after the tragedy the Balinese were like Teletubbies, a children's TV series featuring characters who love each other unconditionally and show their support through frequent hugs. He explained that, like many young Indonesians, his grandchildren watched this program regularly and hence he had equated what he saw with those characters. The Westerners on the other hand were angry, so angry it was difficult to treat many of them. For many Australians the Bali bombing was their first encounter with violent terrorism, and they had difficulties accepting their misfortune at falling victim to such a senseless attack.

We found the following poem taped to the outside window of a Restaurant in Legian. It was in upper-case, bold print, such was the anger. These are just a few lines:

> YOU HURT US BOMBING BALI,
> BUT WE CAN TAKE THE PAIN
>
> BUT IF YOU THINK YOU'LL BEAT US
> YOU CAN THINK A-BLOODY AGAIN
>
> WE BATTLED AT GALLIPOLI
> AND WE FOUGHT THE BLOODY HUN

… and after another 20 lines it finished …

> WE WILL RETURN

There was anger at the fact that pain-management medication had run out at the Sanglah Hospital at 1am on Sunday morning after the bombing. Supplies would have dwindled in any hospital, as no hospital in such a setting could have been prepared for this carnage. But for reasons unknown, the plane from Richmond, east of Sydney, did not arrive until later on Sunday afternoon whereas a flight from Jakarta, where there were ample medical supplies, was less than two hours away. Many people we interviewed queried this time delay and felt it impacted on the death toll. Some broke down in tears, as they expressed their frustration at watching people suffer and being unable to offer relief.

The final death toll has been questioned by several of the people we interviewed in the film. Apparently the Indonesian police only counted the victims from the staff from the Sari Club, Paddy's Bar as well as taxi and truck drivers. Indonesian pedestrians walking along the road on a busy Saturday night were not included, nor were sex workers, beggars and unregistered immigrants, especially those from East Java.

Several months later when filming at Sanglah Hospital, we met a young man with eye and ear injuries who had been walking along the pavement outside Paddy's Bar when the bombing occurred. Although he had long-term health issues from the bombings, he wanted to tell us about his friend. His friend was walking beside him when the bomb exploded and he was reportedly vaporised. There was no body, no clothes, no possessions left behind. The police said, as there was no evidence to prove his friend was dead, he could not be included in the death toll. We heard similar stories several times.

In addition, as the hospitals and clinics in Bali were stretched to the limit on the weekend of the bombing, some Balinese went home to their villages where they died of shrapnel wounds and infected burns. These were injuries that the Balinese had no experience in treating. The deceased were then cremated by the villagers and not included in the final count.

The official count of people killed was 202. Our research showed this was not correct. John was among many who believed there were significantly more Indonesians killed than Australians. Yet the figures published say that of the 202 people killed, 88 were Australians, 38 were Indonesians and the rest were people from more than 20 other nationalities. People in the medical field who were in Bali at the time believed the total number killed was nearer to 350.

We filmed a scene in the famous mountain temple, Pura Batur, which is the hub of an immense network of irrigation temples supplying a large part of Bali's rice farmers' cooperatives (*subak*) with water. From his research in this region, Thomas Reuter spoke of Balinese ideas of the afterlife, and how in Balinese cosmology and ritual practice the spirits of the deceased are sent off to travel along these same water courses down to the sea, until they are purified and invited back to dwell in their family's ancestral shrine, just as water returns from the sea in the form of rain. In this worldview, life is an unending cycle and death does not exist, except as a stage of life.

As the date came closer for the purification ceremony, the number of Westerners in Bali increased. Visitors are always welcomed in Bali. If they make mistakes or if something untoward should happen to them while they are there, many Balinese regard it as their own fault, because they were their guests (*tamu*). Balinese were telling John that the bombings were a message from the Gods indicating they had been neglecting their temples and other religious duties, and had focused too much on material gain. This needed to be rebalanced, with increased time devoted to temple duties and especially by conducting the *Taur Agung* purification ceremony. The Balinese were in fact blaming themselves for the bombings. This is an effective way to overcome the sense of shame that accompanies the idea of being a passive and powerless victim. As John mused one day, 'I wonder how many people in the US blamed themselves for September 11?'

The lead-up to the Purification Ceremony involved the sacrifice of live animals. This was challenging for us to film, but, having seen the size of the destruction the bombing caused, and realising that for the Balinese large offerings to the Gods were needed, we gained acceptance through an understanding of the logic behind this practice. John said the sacrificed animals would be reincarnated favourably, perhaps as human beings. In Balinese villages where the traditional way of life is still strong, almost all meat consumption takes place on festival days and this meat is derived from sacrifices. This signals a respect for life and cultivates an awareness of the sacrifice other creatures make for our benefit.

To film the *Taur Agung*, I was on the beach at Kuta with one of our camera operators, Selene Alcock, and several thousand people. In the oppressive midday heat there was live theatre, dancing and many gamelan percussion orchestras playing. This included a rare and ancient *selunding* orchestra, with the musicians dressed in colourful cloth of deep crimson and gold.

Meanwhile, John, Toby and another camera operator were out on a beautifully decorated fishing boat (*perahu*) about 200 meters from the shore. John had explained that soil was to be brought from the bombsite to the beach, where it would then be handed to the priests who would then board the boats and complete the ceremony out at sea. There were also some live animals to be sacrificed aboard these boats.

John told me the signs to look for that meant the soil was on its way to the beach, and then to relay the information to the crew so they could film. After a moving ceremony where we all knelt and prayed, I watched for signs that the tainted soil was on its way. I was monitoring a small alley for movement and also for signs that the music would recommence. It was of utmost importance that I relay this information so that the filming could recommence. After being on tenterhooks for some time, I noticed the smartly attired players of the ancient gamelan orchestra starting to return. I could also see in the distance the movement of an increasing number of people in the alley. This was the moment to alert the crew.

Quickly I dialled our son's phone and said, 'the *selunding* orchestra players are moving back to their instruments, I can see movement down the alley and the priests are moving towards the boats.' I waited for a response and after a few seconds of delay an unknown male voice replied, 'I think you have the wrong number.' In my haste, I had dialled a complete stranger.

The boats took soil and ashes from the bombsite, along with the priests and live animals. The animals were weighted, so they sank quickly. A large calf was the final animal to be sacrificed and whilst our camera operator was filming his camera stopped working. He later took his camera to Sony, they said they had never seen anything like this before. It was as though a huge electric current had passed through the camera, and all the circuits were melted.

We were fortunate to have two excellent editors, Andrea Lang and Lindi Harrison. Both worked amazingly long hours under trying circumstances whilst dealing with a very emotional subject. During the last seven weeks in Bali we had only three days when we did not work. That was the pace required to meet the deadline for SBS.

Security became a growing issue as unemployment and poverty increased on the island. Our editing room had valuable equipment and so we employed two young Balinese electricians who had been unable to find work since the bombing. They were sons of friends of John's, and when they appeared, they looked very tall, solid and suitably qualified to do the job. I did not realise that Indonesians like to all snuggle up together when sleeping, and one particularly hot night I came down to get a drink of water, to find our tall threatening security guards snuggled up like a couple of teddy bears on the straw floor covering, happily snoring.

A third of the film was now edited and John felt it was coming alive. We were, however, still filming, so as to edit in sections as they happened. This was because grieving for the Balinese is dictated by their religious calendar, and ceremonies must be undertaken on set days.

One Thursday we went to film a very important ceremony with one of the widows from the bombings, Made Kitit, who had put much work into preparing the offerings, all undertaken with great attention to detail. Unfortunately, we arrived at the family temple to find a stray cat had eaten the specially prepared cooked duck that had been placed on the altar. After salvaging as many parts as possible, it was declared not good enough and the family made do with the small pig instead. Next day we looked at the footage, only to realise that in the background was the constant howling of a very annoyed cat that had lost its feast.

Chusnul Chotimah was a woman who was badly burnt on the night of the bomb. After six days she was evacuated to the Royal Perth Hospital, where she spent a month. She suffered severe burns to her face, arms, hands and legs. After surgery she relocated back to Surabaya, Java, with her husband and two young sons. Jenni Ballantyne flew up regularly from Perth to organise and fit Second Skins for burns victims to wear. We established through Jenni that Dr Fiona Wood, a world leading burns specialist (also located in Perth), had asked Chusnul to wear her Second Skin for 22 hours a day. Her skin would then be in the best conditions for the next round of surgery in Perth.

The issue was that Chusnul lived in Surabaya in 33-degree heat and 90 percent humidity, and her Second Skin included a mask that covered her entire face and neck. In addition, she needed to apply cortisone cream, which was required to be kept at temperatures below 25 degrees to remain effective. Chusnul's family owned neither a fridge nor a source of cooling.

Before we flew to Surabaya to interview and film Chusnul, we presented her case along with some footage to groups of NGOs and asked for donations, as she urgently required an air conditioner. Although we attended several swish lunches, no money was forthcoming. Before we flew to Surabaya to film, John, Andrea and I made the decision to buy her an air conditioner. We organised to have it delivered and installed on the day we arrived to film. Chusnul was delighted. The small problem of having no door in the house to contain the cool air was overcome by the camera operator, who paid for one to be installed. In June 2004, a happy Chusnul phoned us in Canberra to say that after three months as a patient at Royal Perth Hospital, she had finished her final burns surgery. She had also completed her rehabilitation and was now returning home.

Haji Agus Bambang had said during his interview, that 'Bali has only got one thing – tourism. If this one thing is not working then a lot of people will go hungry and starve.' Six months later we started to see evidence of this.

Bali has a rich community spirit supported by a communal village system. Prior to the bombings those employed in tourism sent remittances home to their villages, which kept local economies afloat. After the bombings and with the resulting unemployment people retreated back to their villages, and these remittances dried up.

Unfortunately land that had once been available to grow rice and other food crops was now covered with hotels and villas that were empty, as there were no tourists. Also, many of the younger people were trained and employed in tourism and had no experience of farming. Slowly the modest village surplus of food and money started to dry up, and malnutrition began to be an issue.

Sex workers also had a reduced trade. Before the bombings, unprotected sex was the most expensive item. Afterwards it was 'anything goes' as they had so few clients. It was reported this has led to an increase in HIV/AIDS in Bali.

Ni Luh and Warti became widows as a result of the bombs. One Hindu and one Muslim, they forged a deep friendship, based on the recognition that despite their differences, they shared the same destiny as they struggled financially to raise young families without government support. These women were part of the ADOPTA sewing circle set up by a Perth couple, David and Moira, to create an income for the widows.

One of the wonderfully colourful, noisy processions for the widows of the bombing that we filmed involved a 7km walk to make offerings at a local temple. Hundreds of Balinese in temple clothes, from babies to grandparents, carrying brightly coloured umbrellas, were accompanied by several gamelan groups and much noise.

Eventually, the procession was to cross over a bridge and John decided he wanted a shot from the riverbed. John, the camera operator and I rushed ahead of the procession to line up the shot. We ran down the slope, onto the riverbed and started to set up the tripod for the shot. Suddenly, we all realised we were rapidly sinking in thick mud. We were in fact standing in a mangrove swamp. All we could do was laugh, as the procession passed us by, and all we could see was the very top of the brightly coloured umbrellas from our position. Trudging out of the swamp, John declared it a Monty Python moment.

John drew upon his links with his many friends and associates in Bali to locate stories that showed the long history of tolerance on this small island, as a living example to the world. Balinese came to us with stories of the bombing. They knew of John's love for Bali and knowledge of their culture. The Balinese related to him easily and so revealed their inner feelings, knowing that he would respect and value their disclosure.

As our final departure date neared, John was aware of the friendships we had formed, but would have to leave, and so he began putting support structures in place for the people who had worked on the film. John connected Ni Luh and Warti with local businesspeople on the island, who continued to support their sewing endeavours. We tutored one of our translators, who was trained in hospitality, to sit the entrance exam to study tourism at Udayana University in Denpasar. This young man, who has now graduated, is the son of an old friend of John's and is the only person to have ever gone to university from his village.

By 2003, tourist numbers had slowly begun to return to normal. Although the numbers looked the same on paper, the composition was quite different. Tourists were now predominately from Japan, Korea and Taiwan, who came for short stays in the southern part of Bali, and did not travel far afield. This meant that there was still much poverty for those who lived outside this southern area of Bali.

Only 36 hours before we left Bali, we were notified that SBS had given the go-ahead to accept and screen the film on October 12. Following this screening, David Reeve from *Inside Indonesia* wrote, 'This film is about the healing of Indonesia too, and indeed the world. It is expertly crafted and I pay tribute to the power of this film and its expertise.' Bernard Zuel from the *Sydney Morning Herald* wrote, 'There are moments here when you feel you have been punched in the chest. And you will cry.'

Note
1   Further funding later came from a range of other sources and donations.

Going *Below the Wind* with John Darling

Duncan Graham

In the 1990s, television audiences in Britain and Australasia got to see the remarkable story of Indonesia's Sama Bajo. The documentary *Below the Wind* was made by the late Australian director and former Bali resident John Darling. Many years earlier, he'd encountered the sea gypsies of Southeast Asia when shipwrecked on a South Sulawesi island in the 1970s. He called them 'gallant … retiring but daring people' living a hard but 'cheerful and dignified life'.

When Darling heard later that the ocean nomads were being arrested for illegal fishing near Australia, he decided to tell their story. Much footage was shot in Rote, Indonesia's southernmost island in the world's largest archipelago. It seemed the Sama Bajo's traditional lifestyle was doomed.

As a script editor for the film, I went to Rote to investigate.

The title of Darling's documentary *Below the Wind* refers to the name used by the Sama Bajo for the Great South Land, once part of their territory.

But last century Australia got fed up with incursions into its claimed zone. The first laws against 'poachers' were passed in 1906 because the Sama Bajo were said to be 'too industrious'.

No matter that they had been visiting the beaches of northern Australia for at least 600 years. They came to gather trepang, also known as *beche de mer* (French for 'sea-spade') and sea cucumber, though it's a marine animal.

About one million Sama Bajo follow the sea hunter-gatherer tradition across Southeast Asia. Anthropologists believe people in Borneo turned from farming to ranging the seas about 800 AD.

Because few are conventionally religious, the Sama Bajo are sometimes disrespected. In Indonesia, where everyone must belong to one of the six government-approved faiths,[1] the orthodox use derogatory terms which translate as 'spit outs'.

Below the Wind records ceremonies involving placenta being buried at sea and rituals around the slaughter of turtles. According to one interviewee, the Sama Bajo believe the sea is home, a road, food, a friend, a brother and a sister – all enshrined in a genderless spirit called *Oma Medi Lau*.

When Baid Muin saw the cover of the *Below the Wind* video she became a mite emotional. So did her friends who remembered life in distant Sulawesi (see image no. 14).

Yet the photo is bland, just a dark stretch of water lined by stilt houses. In the foreground ripples around an empty prau, known as a lippa-lippa. No people present.

Yet this was once a home for the Sama Bajo. Though not the home. All their resting places are temporary. For maybe twelve centuries they've lived on boats or beaches.

Below the Wind tells of mariners getting land-sick if they spend long periods away from the ocean and recounts their proverb: Fish today, food tomorrow. Sow today, food in six months.

That's changing as the advantages of a more stable life offer attractions: vegetables to break the monotony of fish and rice, education for the kids, consumer goods, and satellite television to entertain while the men spend days – and sometimes weeks – away.

In South Sulawesi fish stocks were getting low and the Sama Bajo's shacks overcrowded. So they scanned the seascape for a new mooring among Indonesia's 17,000 islands.

The landless Sama Bajo are the poorest people in the region and have to settle wherever they're accepted. Till recently they've ignored national borders, building on beaches from the Sulu Archipelago in the northern Philippines, to Malaysia.

With no maps, GPS or compasses, using only inherited encyclopaedic knowledge of stars and winds, swells and tides, one small group navigated their tiny shallow-draught craft a thousand kilometres from South Sulawesi to Papela on the northeast coast of Rote.

The island is in Indonesia's most eastern province, Nusa Tenggara Timur. Jakarta is 2,000 kilometres to the west – Darwin 800 kilometres to the south.

The Sama Bajo had been to the long and narrow island of Rote before, but only for short stays. Much of the island's 1200km^2 landscape is rangeland scrub used by cattle. When around a hundred Sama Bajo arrived in 1990, few locals were concerned.

'Why should we be worried?' asked the *Bupati* (Distict Head) of Rote. 'We welcome them. We've given them certificates for land, helped them with housing and built an ablution block.

'Rote is for all Indonesians, not just the people of Rote, just as all Indonesia is for us. They are Muslim and most on Rote are Catholics and Protestants. As long as people respect each other's culture there's no problem.'

When reminded that countries like Fiji have been ripped by conflict between Indigenous people and latecomers who stayed, expanded and became politically and economically powerful, he shot back: 'That's Fiji – not Indonesia.'

The *Kia* (spiritual leader) at Papela emphasised that there were no tensions with the local people; the immigrants' village and graveyard is separate from the Christians who sail bigger boats from a port nearby.

He said there were about 300 members of his community representing three generations since the first fleet.

The kids originally filmed look fit and lively despite (or because of) their limited diet. Their descendants also appear well; there were no bloated stomachs or xylophone chests obvious, though proper inquiries by health professionals might disclose deficiencies.

Hearing problems have been reported because the men dive deep to scavenge for shells and trepang. Women plaster their faces with *burak*, a ground rice and herb powder to counter sunburn.

Medical research suggests ocean fare reduces the chances of strokes and heart attacks because fish contain Omega 3 fatty acids.

The Sama Bajo men are small and lean, apart from *Haji* (a Muslim who has made the pilgrimage to Mecca) Thosin. 'We [Rotenese] have assisted them, but they have also helped us,' he said. 'For example, they have taught us new fishing techniques.'

When seeking the glistening blue-black 'baby tuna', known in the West as 'bullet tuna', the Sama Bajo set 300-meter lines using multiple hooks decorated with chicken feather lures. Before the newcomers local fishers favoured single hooks and bait.

They work from light one- or two-man *lippa-lippa* (a term also used by northern Australia Aboriginal people for canoes) and fish about ten nautical miles offshore. They report no shortage of stock and return with catches of fifty or more.

Survival at sea depends on remembering, watching and analysing the most subtle moods of sea and season. Where peasants see swells, seafarers see roads. The Sama Bajo read nature like religious scholars scan ancient scrolls.

Once the mountains dip below the horizon there are no landmarks. No life jackets, flares or radios, just wits and wisdom to stay safe.

Though *Below the Wind* shows sturdy construction underway in Papela, only battered remnants of their beach shacks remain, thatched with *lontar* leaves and propped by bleached posts.

Much has changed since Darling uncapped his lens. Some families in Papela have now moved a few meters inland where they live in rough cement-block homes with corrugated iron roofs. In a small market women sell surplus tuna at Rp 15,000 (US $1.10) a kilo.

'Because there's no cold store we cannot preserve the catch,' said Haji Thosin, 'So unless there are many buyers, we have to accept whatever is offered or dry the fish we don't sell.'

Trepang are used in Chinese cooking and medicine. They are sea-floor scavengers surviving on rotting fish and plants. Enthusiasts claim they have healing and aphrodisiac qualities, though this belief may have more to do with the creature's phallic shape rather than any vitamin values.

In 1981 Indonesia agreed that the Australian Fishing Zone be expanded to 320km offshore. Australia gained around 80 per cent of the sea between the two nations' shorelines and set about creating total exclusion.

For a while traditional fishers, meaning sail-only craft, were allowed to continue dropping their lines in a specified area. But when bigger boats (not necessarily crewed by Sama Bajo) started ferrying Middle East asylum seekers, the Australian government got tough, arresting and imprisoning crewmen who ventured too far, confiscating and burning their vessels.

Without GPS the Sama Bajo say they don't know if they've been blown over the imagined border. 'We don't have problems now with the Australians,' said Haji Thosin. 'Embassy officials have been here and agreed we are not deliberately breaking their laws. We've won!'

Being a Sama Bajo is to sail with tragedy. Locals said that three years ago three boats went missing in a storm. No alerts were sounded, no search organised. Twenty men just failed to return and no bodies were recovered.

'This is a village of widows,' Baid Muin said. 'There's one man for every three women and many fatherless children.'

The tone of *Below the Wind* is resigned sadness, an acceptance of the inevitable erosion of an ancient culture and lifestyle by the assaults of modernity.

Darling believed the shortage of fish, Australian hostility and economic upheavals would sink the Sama Bajo's traditional ways, beliefs and values. But the killer wave was always going to be interference by bureaucrats.

These ocean wanderers don't carry passports. They have no permanent abode, no address for government mail, no bank accounts. Few have birth certificates. Census officials find the Sama Bajo impossible to compartmentalise.

They can't remember when they came. They may have been here for years but might all sail away tomorrow. They speak a strange language. Are they even citizens?

In Malaysia some have been forced onto the land. In Australia they are classified as illegal immigrants and put in detention, or called poachers and jailed, their boats burned .

Darling believed he was recording an epilogue for Indonesia's Sama Bajo, but two decades later the Sama Bajo still survive. Maybe this is because the resilient Sama Bajo have adapted to change, fish prices have risen and stocks stabilised. In addition they navigated wisely, steering clear of Australia and making landfall among the tolerant folk of Rote.

This is a revised version of an article first published in The Jakarta Post – J Plus *on 13 August 2016, available at http://indonesianow.blogspot.com/2016/08/gallant-retiring-daring-sama-bajo.html. The author thanks Bupate of Rote for land transport and hospitality.*

Note

1. The six government approved faiths are Islam, Protestantism, Catholicism, Hinduism, Buddhism and Confucianism

Johnny Darling at Murdoch

By Toby Miller

Johnny Darling cut a dashing, dandyish figure through Fremantle and Murdoch University from the moment he arrived in 1990 to work with several filmmakers – including me (unbeknownst in advance to either of us). The late, distinguished Australian media historian Tom O'Regan had told me about John Darling, building him into an imposing, intimidating, spectral presence, a famous director turning his hand to teaching. This rhetoric reached the point where I didn't want to meet the guy when we both arrived in WA. Fame turns me off unless I encounter it accidentally.

That 1990 winter in Perth, Johnny wore knitted suits. They seemed to have acquired a musty smell during his time in hotter climes, and they stood out as much in Western Australia as they would have in Indonesia. You had to like this. And the fact that, despite his fame, Johnny needed a lot of care – and was himself full of caring love. He was vulnerable and strong in equal parts (as if this were an internet-dating profile). He soon became one of my best friends, willing me and others like me to be better each day and in every way.

Both proud and modest, Johnny wanted the best for others, and wanted the best in himself to be recognised. He said, 'Some people would call me an adventurer' and 'There are still people who can remember games I played at centre half-forward for ANU.' Just as relevantly, he loved and admired less conventional forms of success – *Lempad of Bali* and the *Triptych* ultimately mattered more to him than his commercial, scholarly, or sporting ventures.

And Johnny was laden with optimism. He hoped Bill Clinton's election in 1992 presaged a huge change in world politics. As he put it to me, 'He's the first one of our generation to get elected'. Johnny had a touching faith in that oleaginous lounge lizard's links to the counter-culture, neglecting the neoliberal hold of Blue-Dog Democrats and the baleful influence they would wield over the party for decades to come. Despite such gnomic pronouncements, Johnny could accept pinpricks of his occasional pomposity, and even set himself up for them, laughing in anticipation of their delivery. In my estimation, students loved him, as did his colleagues.

Murdoch and teaching

Murdoch University is a fragile yet ongoing project. Set in play during the final, heady days of the Keynesian economic miracle that so favoured the Global North, the school opened its doors just as oil-price shocks, ongoing recession, and an intellectual and public-policy conversion to neoclassical economics were turning Australia from a white working man's paradise to a nation on the lookout for new economic crises as much as its established Euro-isolationism.

Murdoch has been seriously threatened with extinction and amalgamation on numerous occasions from its 1970s emergence to the present. In part this was due to the prevailing political economy, in part because it lacked the alumni base of the ruling class guaranteeing philanthropy, networking, and media coverage, and finally due to the absence of professional schools that produce income (Miller, 2015).

When Johnny and I were there in the early 1990s, many of our students were first-generation in college, or mature folks returning to study. It was a far cry, therefore, from his elite educational experiences as a student. He embraced that difference with vigour, rigor and aplomb.

We taught a documentary class with the noted filmmaker, Mitzi Goldman.[1] The three of us spent many nights gleefully debating culture at his place and other venues. Johnny filmed a documentary, which I assume was never released, about an academic conference in Fremantle. He said afterwards that the event lacked action but overflowed with narcissism. Not the best occasion for an ethnographic filmmaker keen on motion, colour, rhythm, and rhyme.

Johnny's theories of film were alive both to the need for action, for events in front of the camera, to hold our attention; and to the value and technique of the continuity system, emblematically developed by the Hollywood studios before the Second World War but equally prized in mainstream documentary. I recall fondly when he and Mitzi responded incredulously to my saying how much I enjoyed watching the camera regress from an extreme close-up by zooming out. They regarded this as inartistic. I had spoken a heresy. No forgiveness was required. Not least because they were both taken with the avant-garde and with disobeying cardinal commercial virtues.

Johnny was keen on expanding audiences to his work and that of his students, which meant he was always looking to television distribution. That involved a trade-off between an artistic aesthetic and a commercial one. It meant acknowledging the established rituals of a European,

SBS, or ABC commissioning editor, and their preferences for realism and naturalism – for documentaries that came from somewhere in particular, in terms of narration, but also told a story with a recognisable beginning, middle, and end, in that order. Johnny admired the more artisanal, alternative mode of filmmaking, but saw the need to ensure that eager students learnt skills that made their films marketable, watchable and understandable.

Bali and Ethnography

Although history had been his major at ANU and Oxford, Johnny saw himself as an ethnographic filmmaker. This led to some interesting dilemmas when he entered academia full-time at Murdoch. First, there were splits within Asian Studies, of a kind that is quite common – political economy versus cultural studies. One side argued for classic capitalist trends in development, the other for the relative autonomy of aesthetic and quotidian life from the prevailing mode of production. Johnny was in the latter camp, even though he respected the Marxist perspective. In his view, it might have helped explain the general direction of power and control in Indonesia, but it didn't really assist his efforts to comprehend and document daily rituals of art and co-existence.

Second, anthropology and literary studies were being subjected at that time to powerful critiques of Orientalist conduct and perspectives. The postcolonial movement within cultural studies exacted a toll on the careers and life worlds of many, even as it opened up space for new voices, old but neglected ones, and for those without the taint of Cold-War area studies or white-guy heroism entering the jungle for a few snatched weeks each year, or writing about the literatures of countries they had never lived in.

The early 1990s marked a high point of Edward Said's influence in criticising white fetishes of the other (1994), but also of Jim Clifford and George Marcus's critique of anthropology (1986). There were simultaneous stirrings of a political-economic opposition to Clifford Geertz's move towards the relative autonomy of culture from economics (1973).

Geertz had been a supporter of Johnny's and influenced him considerably. The counter-Geertzian tendency included a powerful formation at Murdoch, spearheaded by Dick Robison's Marxist critique of Indonesia's clientelist oligarchy and its exploitation of natural resources and finance capital (1986).[2] While Johnny could see value in blending materialism with cultural criticism to explain Indonesia, as per Benedict Anderson's work, he was proud and willing to line up alongside Geertz and his quasi-functionalist focus on symbols.

That bifurcation of political economy versus culturalism became very pointed after we had both departed from WA. The 1998 overthrow of the Suharto regime in Indonesia, driven by the previous year's regional financial crisis and a restive civil society, made Geertz look misguided, especially when his regular welcome under Suharto was juxtaposed with Anderson's three decades of exile from Indonesia during the murderous, authoritarian anti-leftism that followed the attempted coup in 1965. The US foreign-policy establishment and its mouthpiece, *The New York Times*, continued to regard that event, which cost up to a million Marxists and fellow-travellers their lives, as something pacific and cultural rather than brutal and animated by Cold-War ideology and geopolitics. The paper relied on Geertz as a key source, neglecting social movements (Kristof, 1998; Shernon, 1998).

We know now how profoundly the CIA influenced US communication and area studies throughout the Global South from the 1950s in the name of development and political stability (of a sort). We know this both from Anderson's memoir of the poisonous, poisoning, yet productive field of Southeast Asian political science at Cornell and the Social Sciences Research Council that was, David H Price's excavation of anthropologists' complicity, and Christopher Simpson's excoriating revelations about how the doxa of political communication were dispatched from North Atlantic seminar rooms to Third World oligarchies (Anderson, 2016; Price, 2016; Simpson, 1994). But much of this was rumour when we were together at Murdoch.

Johnny was susceptible to many of the critiques adumbrated above, because of the life he had led, his self-presentation (as if he were of the gentrified poor) and the subject matter of his art. Sometimes he felt wounded by the negativity of such tendencies. But after decades as a resident of Indonesia, working collaboratively with local intellectuals and artists, he was not really a target – more someone who felt keenly denunciations directed in part at people he had known, or whose work he valued.

Whilst he felt the force of anti-Orientalist concerns, Johnny was neither cowed by nor dismissive of them. He was not defensive. He stood up for what he believed in and had done, but always found time to listen to opposing viewpoints, endorse many of them, and seek new ways of collaboration. Sometimes he was mildly irritated by Olympian remarks made by people who had not spent as long as he had learning about, working with, and archiving the lives of others; but he was, above all, driven by engagement and respect.

Unlike most such critics – but not Said himself – Johnny loved and gathered antiquarian books galore in his donnish home, along with an array of herbs and complementary treatments for maladies, and an endless diversity of teas, which were as carefully categorised as his books. I can still recall the aromas and mustiness of his study, blending all these elements like an aged curiosity shop.

When I got the opportunity to move to New York in 1993, Mitzi and Johnny unabashedly urged me to do so, just as they had encouraged me to apply for a job there, convinced, as I was not, of my candidacy – in fact, seemingly certain I'd get an offer. When I left, we were only occasionally in touch, due to the distance and the prevailing state of electronic communication.

When his devoted, creative wife Sara told me of his final illness in late 2011, I wrote this to him, through her:

> Johnny, I love you and have loved you from the day we met. You have been, from that first moment of knowing you, an incredible inspiration to me personally, professionally, intellectually, politically – you name it. And you love cricket and football (though not the Tigers, regrettably).
>
> You warmly and generously introduced me to your marvellous parents. Meeting your dad and dining with him remains a highlight of my life.
>
> You always encouraged and valued my work and wanted to stretch and develop my ideas when we worked together. Both when we taught classes and when we just talked in your place in Perth, life was always going somewhere good, always headed in a positive and exciting direction, albeit with a cutting critical edge.
>
> In the many years since we've been in daily touch, a month hasn't gone by that I haven't thought about those days. When I was hoping to move to Gotham, you (and Mitzi) encouraged me as no others did. You told me I could do it, that this was the right canvas for me.

Right now, as you may recall, I live in Mexico, after several years in LA. I am a bit of an exile here, though happily so. You know all about that as a world traveller and someone who has lived all over Australia, too. The voluntary exile's experience is both rich and poor, as you taught me with your Balinese and Oxford stories.

… I love and admire your films, which I have taught to appreciative audiences around the US. I loved going to the cricket with you, talking about Gary Ablett, discussing your lustrous times at the 'G', hearing about your days playing (I think) centre-forward for the ANU, or maybe on the flank.[3] You once told me 'There are people who can still remember games I played.' I loved your companionship, unfailing support, inspiring friendship, and constant desire to challenge and encourage; but above all, I loved your art and ideas.

It's many years since we've been together, and I know you and yours are suffering greatly. As I hope the words above show, my recollection and joy at our past together are undimmed (my memory may be partially inaccurate, of course, given the dissolute life I led before, during, and after those times).

To return to where I began, Johnny, you have been and remain a great friend. In the period since we spent day after day together, I have always known I could count on you in a crisis or to uplift me with your art. I love you and am honoured and happy that we share the history we do.

Best

Toby

My final compelling memory of Johnny is of a day at the cricket together in early 1992, at a now-abandoned Test venue: the concrete WACA, close to downtown Perth. He smiled and laughed and loved being – it was his very heaven. Given Johnny's background, he could have lived an existence full of little else. But a yearning for difference and self-development led him beyond the ease of well-off white life. That search for meaning was far more profound than glorified tourists or apparatchiks masquerading as ethnographers. He went and lived it.

Notes

1. See https://goodpitch2australia.com.au/team/dr-mitzi-goldman/.
2. These were not absolute binary oppositions. Dick drew on Geertz's research that looked at political economy, prior to the latter's conversion to textualism.
3. John was a fanatical supporter of the Geelong Football Club. The 'G' refers (probably) to the Melbourne Cricket Ground (MCG) the major stadium of Australian Rules Football. Australian Rules is (for the benefit of non-Australian readers) a different game to both soccer (known in Europe as football and in Indonesia as sepak bola) and rugby. Gary Ablett was a famous player of the 1980s and 1990s, playing mostly for Geelong. Centre-forward and 'the flank' are positions on the field usually held by strong and accurate kickers of the ball.

References

Anderson, Benedict, *A Life Beyond Boundaries*, London:, Verso, 2016.
Clifford, James and Marcus, George (eds.), *Writing Culture: The Poetics and Politics of Ethnography*, Berkeley, University of California Press, 1986.
Geertz, Clifford, *The Interpretation of Cultures: Selected Essays*, New York, Basic Books, 1973.
Kristof, Nicholas D., 'Suharto, a King of Java Past, Confronts Indonesia's Future', *New York Times* 17 May 1998, available via subscription from https://www.nytimes.com/1998/05/17/world/suharto-a-king-of-java-past-confronts-indonesia-s-future.html.
Miller, Toby, 'Murdoch's Trajectory: From Periphery to Core; From Core to Periphery?' *Murdoch Voices: The First 40 Years at Murdoch University*, Bolton, Geoffrey (ed.), Perth, Murdoch University, 2015, 88–93.
Price, David H., *Cold War Anthropology: The CIA, the Pentagon, and the Growth of Dual Use Anthropology*, Durham, Duke University Press, 2016.
Robison, Richard, *Indonesia: The Rise of Capital*, Sydney, Allen & Unwin, 1986.
Said, Edward, *Culture and Imperialism*, New York, Vintage Books, 1994.
Shernon, Philip, 'Of the Turmoil in Indonesia and its Roots', *New York Times*: B9, 9 May 1988.
Simpson, Christopher, *Science of Coercion: Communication Research and Psychological Warfare, 1945–1960*, New York, Oxford University Press, 1994.

Bleaching Australia

Graeme MacRae

While John is best known for his life and work in Indonesia, he never saw himself as an exile, and he remained deeply Australian, in ways that ranged from lifelong passions for cricket and Australian Rules Football (especially the Geelong team) to voracious daily consumption of Australian newspapers, his late-blooming career as a painter of Australian landscapes and a deep concern for the treatment, past and present of Indigenous Australians. All his Indonesian films were, in various ways, directed to Australians, to explain to them something about the neighbour they at best misunderstood and at worst, mistrusted and feared. This mission of cultural diplomacy was most explicit in *Below the Wind*, which began with the one-sided war waged by the Australian Coast Guard on Indonesian fishermen straying into Australian waters, and returned periodically to this and to the prehistorical connections between the peoples of northern Australia and Indonesian seafarers and collectors of *trepang*.

After his return to Australia in 1987, John lived in Sydney, supporting himself by short-term and part-time teaching jobs, while exploring ideas for films, including a television series on the Indian Ocean provisionally titled East of Zanzibar with ABC journalist Jack Pizzey, with whom had worked on *Slow Boat to Surabaya* and a film on the Australian artist Ian Fairweather who had lived in various parts of Asia including Bali. In 2001 John and Sara moved to Canberra where John was a Visiting Fellow in the Research School of Pacific and Asian Studies, at the Australian National University. This was at the height of what were known as the History Wars – a highly polarised public debate over the mode of colonisation of Australia and especially interpretations of the nature and extent of violence against Indigenous Australians in this process. John became intensely interested in this debate and he began research for a film based on it. In 2005, Taman Sari productions worked with Andrew Pike of Ronin Films, on applications for funding for a film provisionally titled *Bleaching Australia*. It was designed to use the History Wars as a framework but to insert into the debates the previously silenced Indigenous voices to create a sustained two-way juxtaposition of cross-cultural differences of representation of the entire history of post-contact Australia. Like all of John's films, it was envisaged as a multi-layered tapestry of images, voices and media – including such ironic and black-humorous innovations as an Indigenous interpretation of the story of the 'Three little pigs' and a role-reversed re-enactment of Cook's landing in 1770.

It was described in the funding applications as a feature-length film or a pair of films designed for one-hour television slots (presumably depending on the funding found), but either way designed to span commercial, television and educational markets. The ambitious scope outlined in the funding documents seems (looking at them two decades later) to demand a substantially longer format, and aspects of its approach anticipated that of the celebrated series *First Australians* made around the same time for SBS television, and also John Pilger's later film, *Utopia*. John also envisaged linking the film to an online database of 'footnotes' – archival material documenting the evidence on which the film is based – an innovation later realised in the posthumously released *Lempad of Bali* ebook.

By late 2006, a revised version of the same document was tighter, more focused and probably more realistic in scope. But it also reflected considerable development in John's thinking about the film, aiming to provoke a reflexive response in the viewer by incorporating John's reflection on own family history and the role of Geelong Grammar School in perpetuating a white version of the history of western Victoria.

Some funding was obtained from the Australian Film Commission and the Bushell Foundation, to develop the idea, but because of John's declining health at this time, he and Sara moved to Melbourne for better access to treatment and the project never developed beyond this stage.

Bleaching Australia may be seen on one hand as 'another great film that didn't happen', but the ideas are clear enough that it can be seen as more than that. In the trajectory of John's career it represents a closing of the circle, returning (like John Pilger in *Utopia*) to his roots, in Australia, in its conflicted colonial history, but also to the contradictions of his own position in that history.

Part III

Indonesia:
A True Home

John Darling and I Gusti Made Sumung

Bruce W. Carpenter

A note from Graeme MacRae

In John's first film, Lempad of Bali, *the real star is Lempad's son, I Gusti Made Sumung,*[1] *speaking directly to the camera and engaging the audience, but also, behind the scenes, the dalang (master puppeteer) driving the making of the film. Making this film was a high point in Gusti Sumung's long career as one of the key figures in the complex relationship between Bali and its foreign visitors through the twentieth century.*

Gusti Sumung was born around 1916. His friendships with foreigners began in the late 1920s, with Walter Spies, followed soon after by Margaret Mead, Gregory Bateson and Jane Belo. Sixty years later I had the privilege of being the last of his long line of foreign friends. But in the middle, his longest, most productive and I believe most important friendship was with John Darling, for whom he was 'my closest friend – my Balinese father [...] a remarkable man [...] I could not have asked for a better teacher or wiser friend.'

I arrived in Bali in 1993 and within weeks my family were living in a wonderfully rambling but decrepit house Gusti Sumung had built years before to house his foreign friends. He died shortly before my departure in mid-1994. During that final year of his life, he became my guide and mentor. He seemed to relish one final friendship with a foreigner who reminded him of his friends of earlier years, all of whom he compared favourably but wistfully with the new breed of tourists. And in between, was John.

Much of my research consisted of long trips, in the valley upstream from Ubud, mostly on foot – village-to-village, temple-to-temple. Gusti Sumung approved of this method but advised me to wear sarong and udeng (headcloth) as signs of respect for tradition. He himself rarely wore udeng, but always a simple sarong. He insisted that this was proper Indonesian clothing and lamented his own early years of wearing long trousers in imitation of Western/modern sartorial style. After each excursion I would report my discoveries to him. He asked detailed questions and made cryptic comments. He never told me where to go or what to do, he just made subtle suggestions and let me know when I'd got it right. He never answered my questions directly, but with stories from which I had to distil my own meanings.

Years later, reading through John's archives, I discovered that I had been retracing many of the very trips that John and Gusti Sumung had made together, also on foot, twenty years earlier. Gusti Sumung's detailed knowledge and his network of contacts, came from his years as sedehan *(collector of land taxes) in this area, and wherever I went up that valley his name was the best calling card, guaranteeing a warm welcome.*

But by the time I knew him, Gusti Sumung knew his days were numbered. He was concerned about the knowledge and stories that would be lost, but also the things that would be added and misrepresented. This was part of why people like John and I were so important to him.

Gusti Sumung had eight children, seven of them sons. They are all quite different and have taken different paths in life. I see parts of Gusti Sumung in all of them, as if he has split into seven parts – a notion not inconsistent with Balinese ideas of the reincarnation of great people. Among these sons, one, Gusti Nyoman Sudara, has inherited something of the artistic talents of his grandfather Lempad – especially as a painter and carver of masks used in ritual. Of Lempad's own children, only one, Gusti Sumung's younger sister was a talented painter. Others of the younger generations are also painters.

Another of Gusti Sumung's foreign friends from the same period was Bruce Carpenter, connoisseur, collector and Indonesian art historian, who co-ordinated a major book about I Gusti Nyoman Lempad in 2014.[2] Here is his story of Gusti Sumung in earlier years.

John Darling, Gusti Made Sumung and Gusti Nyoman Lempad

When John Darling arrived on Bali in the early 1970s, the island was on the cusp of great cross-cultural experiment that would have far-reaching consequences. At the time, neither John nor any of the eclectic collection of young people who had arrived from across the world, of which I was one, had any clear plan or purpose. Refugees of the international youth movement that had filled our generation with naive dreams of blazing new paths and paradigms, we found Bali a fecund setting suspended somewhere between the profound mysticism of the East and the tropical exoticism of Polynesia to indulge our fantasies and dreams.

We also saw ourselves as heirs of an earlier generation of seekers, artists, vagabonds, eccentrics and scholars, especially the legendary figure of Walter Spies, who had flocked to Bali in the 1930s. As then, the Balinese were gracious hosts, but also adept at role-playing – not to deceive but to please. We projected upon them god-like qualities, a perfect race on a perfect island that lived in harmony with nature, creativity and spirituality. For us the island was an addictive drug we could not get enough of. We were in bliss, at least, until the money ran out and our visas expired.

With few opportunities to earn money, even if we were qualified, we scrambled to re-invent and establish ourselves. John, who had the advantage of arriving early, was lucky and particularly clever at sensing opportunity. It did not take him long to survey the landscape and form an alliance with the family of I Gusti Nyoman Lempad, a prominent artist.

Truth be told, the Lempad family was also in need of an ambassador at a point when their fortunes were fading. Lempad had been one of the major figures in the extraordinary creative efflorescence of Balinese art that resulted in the rise of the Pita Maha Movement in the 1930s. But the Second World War, the Indonesian struggle for independence, political instability, natural disaster, economic hardship and finally the bloody aftermath of the fall of President Sukarno and rise of Suharto's New Order government only a few years before John's arrival – all meant that tourists stayed away for almost three decades. This was disastrous for Balinese artists, including Lempad.

The situation was further complicated by Lempad's advanced age, for he was well beyond his prime, and was being eclipsed by a new generation of artists painting in new styles at the same time that his largely Dutch former patrons were growing old, fading and fast disappearing. John's interest in Lempad, and in Balinese art and culture, greatly pleased I Gusti Made Sumung, Lempad's eldest son. His father's right-hand man and the de facto head of the family, Gusti

Sumung was a notable figure in his own right despite having inherited none of his father's artistic talents.

Because of his father's friendships with the expatriate community, the young Gusti Sumung was exposed to the circle of often-famous Westerners and he attended a series of elite schools where he learned Indonesian, Dutch and English. Later he became the private secretary of Jane Belo, an anthropologist who worked with Margaret Mead. Sumung understood the benefits of working with Westerners and was comfortable dealing with them. Although John and those who followed were different from our pre-war predecessors, we formed useful and symbiotic relationships with local artists.

Most of us had a tendency to exaggerate the importance or extent of our relationships. I have heard many intimate that they had direct, meaningful communications with Lempad himself. My own experience during several visits to the Lempad compound was that the old man lived in cocoon of his own making. At the time I perceived this as a mystical state of consciousness.[3] When Lempad made brief appearances he spent most of his time sitting silently. Photos from the time reveal he was a frail old man of great age. On rare occasions a family member would whisper into his ear. Even if we could hear these inaudible exchanges, at most we had only a basic grasp of the complex Balinese language, which was the only one spoken by Lempad. My conclusion is that when people talk of meeting Lempad from the late 1960s until his death in 1978, this only meant they may have been in his presence. Any and all words spoken came through I Gusti Made Sumung, who I nicknamed the gatekeeper in an essay in the Lempad of Bali book[4]. I have no reason to believe John was any different in this matter although he clearly spent the most time with the family.

It did not take long before the name John Darling became synonymous with that of the Lempad family and quickly expanded to the Ubud School of Balinese art. John's circle of friends included several fellow Australians from Sydney who had 'gone native' – the flamboyant painter Jan van Wieringen, who settled on the Sayan ridge near Ubud; the then little-known landscape architect, Michael White, better known as Made Wijaya, of whom all of us were jealous at his ability to quickly gain a remarkable fluency in Balinese. Another member was the perennial bad-boy artist-musician Shane Sweeney who claimed he had grown up in a circus. It was he who later coined the term Bule Aga in the late 1980s to describe the original old boys club of the early period. This was a pun on the Bali Aga people of Bali who claim to have been the original inhabitants with Bali but replaced by *bule*, a slightly derogatory term for albinos also applied to white foreigners. Others in his inner circle included the filmmakers, Lawrence and Lorne Blair and photographer Rio Helmi. Then came the scholars both established and budding including Hedi Hinzler, Michel Picard, Carol Warren, Adrian Vickers, Margaret Wiener and later still others including Graeme MacRae and Thomas Reuter.[5]

My wife Carola and I first met John in Ubud where we began living for extended periods of time in the mid-1970s. Not surprisingly we became active participants in the various social activities of Ubud's still small expatriate community, which John often attended. My old friend, French scholar Michel Picard, aka 'Handsome Pierre', made my first official introduction. My only qualifications at the time were a deep interest in Southeast Asian culture and a broad education in art history. At the time I was preoccupied with the theory of human archetypes especially as seen in Balinese theatre and shadow puppetry.

I still have a razor-sharp memory of John, his red hair, aquiline nose, pale eyes and pale complexion. Lanky, thin and usually taciturn, he seemed to be shy and very cerebral. Usually huddled with his friends, I noted that he was quick of tongue and had an often-wicked sense of humour, especially around his Australian compatriots who had their own peculiar lingo. When the subject changed to Balinese art and culture, however, his demeanour changed rapidly assuming a more serious tone that mirrored the authority of a schoolmaster. The irony that he may have been unconsciously mirroring the behaviour of his father was not lost on me, particularly because everyone knew that his father was not happy with his son's life choices, a condition many of us shared with him. While he was, at times, overly didactic and with a penchant for myths, poetic digressions and pop mysticism, I much appreciated his insights and imagined him as a latter-day Romantic poet à la Percy Shelley. Despite his refined exterior I also sensed that, like all of us, he believed he was a man with a mission, driven by the need to prove himself.

One of the most memorable meetings Carola and I had with John was in Amsterdam in 1979. John, who was in the company of Lorne Blair, with whom he had made the brilliant film *Lempad of Bali*, was there to help organise a major exhibition of Balinese art at the Tropical Museum, entitled *Walter Spies and Balinese Art* (1980). Sitting on the terrace of the American Hotel on Leidseplein on a chilly but sunny autumn afternoon, wrapped in a wool pullover and jacket, John seemed ethereal, especially next to the physicality of the far more robust Lorne. To our delight we both found the normally reserved John friendly and gregarious as we drank Wiener Melanges.[6]

My impression was that both of them were happy to meet friends from Bali after an extended and somewhat isolated sojourn in Holland as the guest of Hans Rhodius, who was at the time the biggest collector of Walter Spies and author of his first major biography. Carola and I knew Hans, who was a member of an old and respectable colonial family from her hometown of Haarlem. We were surprised when John and Lorne, who found out he was also gay, expressed a fear that he might sneak into their rooms at night! To prevent any mishap they told a hilarious tale about putting chairs beneath the doorknobs of their rooms. Carola and I, who knew the very formal and already elderly Rhodius, assured them that they were safe.

It was a good moment for John and Lorne, who were both proud and buoyed by the critical acclaim with which *Lempad of Bali* was being received. Despite its sometimes non-factual assertions (that Indonesia became independent in 1949 for example),[7] *Lempad of Bali* stands as a compelling and important documentary of great beauty. For many of us it was a mirror that not only paralleled our own personal experiences in Bali, but also pioneered a new and intimate approach to Balinese art and culture that belonged to our generation.

John was also proud to have been invited to write an essay on Balinese art for the forthcoming exhibition's catalogue.[8] At a certain moment our conversation focused on a subject that many of us had been rethinking – that the brilliance of the Pita Maha Movement art was foremost the direct result of the creative genius of Balinese artists, and that the prevailing story of a Balinese renaissance created by the benevolent intervention of Western artists was false and colonialist. If asked to single out John's greatest contribution to the history of Balinese art, I would say it was his clear elucidation of this truth in this essay.

Over the next years, Carola and I would spend more and more time in Bali and grow increasingly close to Gusti Sumung. As with John and those, like Michel Picard and Graeme MacRae, who followed, he gladly took on the role as our guide and mentor in multifaceted ways. It was a time of adventure and exploration when a small circle of us were determined to see the best Balinese performances in their natural settings. Gusti Sumung was not only our top informant but also often accompanied us. Departing early evening in a motorcycle cavalcade, we would drive indeterminate distances often on dirt roads to remote villages. New moons were particularly challenging at night at a time when there were no street lamps, as well as wailing packs of dogs and numerous road hazards. More than once we skirted disaster. I remember returning home one chilly night from a mountain village with Gusti Sumung sitting behind me on a rickety 70cc motorbike when I struck a deep hole and nearly fell. Breathing deeply I was able to avoid tumbling. I felt honoured to be carrying a man old enough to be my grandfather and felt his bright but frail presence. It was my sacred duty to deliver him home safe.

While getting there and back was often challenging, upon arrival we were mesmerised by the ancient and, to us, profound grandeur of what we saw. With no electricity and magnificent backdrops, it was as if we had been transported back in time to a medieval setting. The dances and ceremonies exuded power and meaning even if we were still unfamiliar with the specifics. Each experience was followed by questions and answers from Gusti Sumung, who loved drinking strong, sweet black coffee in small cups as he smoked his beloved unfiltered kretek cigarettes.

In 1981 Gusti Sumung helped me research an itinerary for a study group of Americans who wanted to meet genuine Balinese healers and religious figures, led by Dr Stanley Krippner[9] of Saybrook University and myself. It was a remarkable experience, long before Ubud had become a centre of Western healers and spiritual masters. Our meeting with Dr Denny Thong, head of Bali's only psychiatric hospital in Bangli for twenty years, was especially insightful. At the time Dr Thong, who was a well-known and influential character nationally and internationally, provided a wealth of information, as well as some hilarious anecdotes. While on a government trip to the United States he met with Margaret Mead, who took offense at the young doctor who dared challenge her theories about the relationship between Balinese character and schizophrenia. He recalled with a laugh that she not only stormed out of the office in rage but also hit him with her walking cane.

Thong's experience of trying to set up a modern medical system in Bali, where tradition was still so entrenched, convinced him of the need for mental health specialists to familiarise themselves with local beliefs and, where possible, to avoid violating them. Krippner, Thong and I would later produce *Psychiatrist in Paradise*, a biography of his Balinese experience that was finally published in 1993. My task was to identify and interview a selection of Balinese traditional healers and describe their work.

Naturally my guide was Gusti Sumung. Together we visited numerous *balian*, the generic term for healers who ranged from those who went into trance to respected wise men with extensive libraries of sacred palm-leaf manuscripts. The latter, known as *balian usada*, were particularly impressive for their immense knowledge. One day, without announcing where we were headed, Gusti Sumung took me on a stroll through the narrow lanes behind the Lempad compound and introduced me to I Gusti Lingsir,[10] an elderly master of Balinese geomancy (*kosala-kosali*) and a wide variety of magical protective rituals, spells, amulets, oils, unguents and drawings. I would later learn that he was a close member of a family whose wisdom the Lempad family often sought out. I was surprised that Gusti Sumung did not tell me this and wondered if he worried that I would think him superstitious. I also later speculated on the influence and connection between Lempad and the black and white magical drawings known as *rerajahan*.

In the course of visiting scores of healers and magic men and women, Gusti Sumung also introduced me to I Ketut Liyer, who would later gain fame as the mystical teacher of Elizabeth Gilbert, author of *Eat, Pray, Love*. Gusti Sumung described him as a nice fellow and failed painter who billed himself as a wise man and healer after he had read a book about palmistry, which has absolutely nothing to do with Balinese tradition. Virtually anyone who went to him received the same treatment described in Gilbert's book. Gusti Sumung recommended that he be excluded from our book, describing him as a tourist *balian* specialising in middle-aged Western women![11]

Like his father, Gusti Sumung was wiry and thin. Sometimes in a chiaroscuro environment lighted by the golden flickering flames of oil lamps, his chiselled face with overly large eyes took on a mask-like quality that sometimes resembled a skull. A chain smoker of clove cigarettes, he specialised in making puns and poignant witticisms, which ended with a broad mischievous grin. Most of these concerned a clear belief that tradition and the quality of Balinese life were under threat by a new, money-driven economy. Pointing at ugly constructions made of cheap cement cinder blocks, he quipped: 'We Balinese used to build in mud and thatch, now we build with dollars.' Another concerned the correlation between time and activities:

> During the day, the Balinese always worked hard planting their fields, building and all manner of labour. But this would stop after sunset, for the night was the time for dancing, singing,

playing music, making love and sleeping. Today we are ruled by greed and confusion.

Our conversations were usually in Indonesian smattered with English and Balinese words. Carola and Gusti Sumung also developed their own unique relationship, usually speaking in Dutch. While Gusti Sumung's command was somewhat rusty, he was definitely fluent. She also helped him resolve a problem with the payment of his monthly pension, which he still received from the Dutch government. His spoken Dutch also had a special charm because of his use of somewhat archaic idiomatic expressions that were no longer common. Because I also had a good command of Dutch, it often served as a useful emergency tool we could revert to when either of us was unsure of the proper Indonesian or English word. His command of several languages and behaviour also reflected his mental prowess, even though he often preferred playing the role of a simple man, which like a clever farmer he was capable of using to his advantage.[12]

John would periodically have great expectations of more and better opportunities, especially after coming back to Bali from Australia or occasionally further afield. When it came to Balinese art and culture he was certainly on the A-list of who to go to. For those of us who thought the Bali we knew was immutable, change brought by the accelerating pace of tourism was not easy to accept. While these seem insignificant when compared with today's landscape, the morphing of Ubud and other areas from charming, sleepy villages into tawdry tourist traps grated our souls. Gusti Sumung, who complained that Nomad, a popular nightspot opposite the Lempad compound, played loud music and stayed open as late as 9pm, echoed this sentiment! We were also growing older and entering relationships. John surprised most of us when he suddenly arrived with a beautiful wife, the American artist Diana Darling.

Carola and I visited them on several occasions at John's rustic home. It was located at the end of an unpaved road which suddenly dissolved into verdant rice terraces where the Lempad family had given John a piece of land on the edge of a steep ravine to use. On sunny days getting there was not too much of a problem but when it rained the muddy narrow embankments between the rice terraces were slippery and not always stable.

Their bohemian residence was a ramshackle collection of low-lying temporary buildings constructed of bamboo and thatch. Everything was very old-style Balinese including a very primitive mud-brick kitchen. Because it was lower than the fields to the west, the whole seemed particularly soggy during the monsoon. During one visit around 1982, John seemed moody and angry. He was growing increasingly frustrated because of the failure of funding for new and more ambitious projects. From his point of view he was a proven and deserving scholar and filmmaker but funding for his projects was always a problem.

His inhalation of an endless stream of sweet-smelling clove cigarettes followed by wheezing and coughing further enforced my impression of an increasingly depressive atmosphere as time went by. Carola and I were also concerned about his and Diana's conspicuous consumption of a cocktail made of two Balinese liquors, brem, a sweet rice wine, and high-octane arak.[13] Having never felt we were close enough to be frank, we refrained from expressing our worries though we did discuss it with several friends. All agreed that he needed a change. This would come quickly enough, with a tumultuous marital breakup with Diana, who would go on to become a writer and editor in her own right.[14]

We saw less of John during the ensuing period and later learned he had decided to return to Australia to teach.[15] We would meet again on several occasions while he was shooting *Bali Triptych*, which was released in 1988. On one occasion, we sat down together before a dance performance he was preparing to shoot that evening. After directing the placement of lighting, he explained his decision to use only natural light provided by kerosene-powered pressure lanterns when filming at night. As a former cameraman I was fascinated by his attempt to preserve the authenticity of the experience and the intensity of his vision. As John was now resident in Australia, we received only occasional news of his whereabouts and doings from mutual friends. In the transient expatriate community, his absence was only noted by those with long memories.

My final meeting with John occurred after the 2002 Bali bombing, when he was shooting for his final Balinese movie, *The Healing of Bali*. I was especially honoured because he actually came to visit me, a real first. John had heard I had a collection of a number of Lempad and other Pita Maha drawings. I was pleased when he took special interest in a Lempad drawing of the Barong Landung, which was one of my favourites. He even asked me if I would consider selling it to the Australian National Gallery, which according to him did not have any good Lempad artworks. We reminisced on changes, our past experiences and shared our fondness of Gusti Made Sumung, who had passed away in 1994, leaving the Lempad compound somewhat rudderless. On the subject of mortality he told me of his own frightening health challenges. It was a warm encounter, somehow tinged with the realisation that in other circumstances we would have been much closer.

John's memory lingers still after his far too early passing in 2011. It burned particularly bright during the compiling of *Lempad of Bali: The Illuminating Line*, a large volume dedicated to the art of Lempad. It was an idea that had been percolating for many years. I had first discussed it with Gusti Sumung in the late 1980s. The opportunity to make it real would come around 2006 when Soemantri Widagdo, the director of Museum Puri Lukisan, told me of a plan to mount a major retrospective to celebrate the museum's fiftieth anniversary. He asked me to coordinate, co-author and give form to a major book. It was a task that was only fully realised in 2014.

This task was not only a great honour but also a recreation of a past in which John played a dynamic role. It's main title, *Lempad of Bali*, was chosen as homage to John and Lorne's film and work. I also insisted on including an essay from John. Thanks to Sara's generosity, this was possible. As editor I gently revised John's poignant ode to the life of Lempad. The idea was to make it read as if he was reciting it live. Good editing, as any good editor will tell you, requires one to enter into the mind and feelings of the author, a kind of channelling if you like. His essay, like the book and exhibition, was conceived and presented as tribute, firstly to I Gusti Nyoman Lempad, secondly to his son and universal mentor, I Gusti Made Sumung, then to the Balinese people and finally to our comrade in arms, the faithful torchbearer, John Darling.

Notes

1   Gusti is a minor aristocratic title. Balinese, including Gusti Sumung, tend to be quite particular about their titles and I know he would not have approved of me referring to him by his given name only, hence the repetition of Gusti.
2   Carpenter et al., *Lempad of Bali*.
3   Referring to an early period of Japanese occupation and revolution, John Darling described this as a catatonic state in his film on Lempad.
4   Carpenter et al., *Lempad of Bali*.
5   Hedi Hinzler is Professor of Southeast Asian Studies at Leiden University; Michel Picard is a French sociologist, an expert first on tourism and later on religion; Carol Warren is an Australian anthropologist; Adrian Vickers is professor of Asian Studies at Sydney University; Margaret Wiener is an

American anthropologist who worked in Bali in the late 1980s and early 1990s. Graeme MacRae is a New Zealand anthropologist much of whose research has been in Ubud. Thomas Reuter is an Australian/German anthropologist who did pioneering research in highland Bali in the 1990s.

6   A Viennese version of cappuccino.
7   On being reminded of this mistake, John embarrassingly apologised saying he had got the date from a Dutch history book and that it was 'too expensive to change' the narration of the film (eds.). The Dutch always regarded 27 December 1949 as the date when the Dutch parliament transferred sovereignty from the former Netherland Indies to the united states of Indonesia. They did not recognise Soekarno's 17 Augustus 1945 Proclamation of Independence.
8   Hans Rhodius and John Darling, *Walter Spies and Balinese Art* (Amsterdam: Terra, 1980).
9   An American psychologist with an interest in the supernatural edges of human experience.
10 'Gusti Lingsir' means '(very) old Gusti'; in this case it refers to one known as Gusti Lingsir Balian, who was the inspiration for Diana Darling's celebrated novel *The Painted Alphabet*. He was also the father of one of John's friends, Gusti Putu Purna. (See image no. 16, of Gusti Putu Purna holding a photograph that John took of his father).
11 David Stuart-Fox has recently published an excellent book about his own experience of Ketut Liyer during this period: *Pray, Magic, Heal: The Story of Ketut Liyer* (Saritaksu: New Saraswati Press, 2015).
12 When the Japanese invaded Bali in 1942, Gusti Sumung did exactly this – reinventing his sophisticated, western-influenced self as a simple rice farmer. In the process he came to appreciate the beauty and complexity of rice-farming, which led to his post-war career as a *sedehan* (collector of rice-field taxes).
13 A spirit distilled from (usually) *tuak*, a palm beer.
14 Diana Darling's novel, *The Painted Alphabet* (New York: Houghton Mifflin, 1992), is widely regarded as one of the best on Bali by a foreigner.
15 John separated from Diana and returned to Australia in 1987.

Part IV

John Darling:
A Life in Memories

Three Funerals

Graeme MacRae

John was a man of many parts – not easily classified. Was he a filmmaker? A poet? Author? Cultural ambassador? Teacher? Bali expat? Indonesia expert? He was all of these, but he was also a son, brother, friend, lover, husband and, eventually, a father and grandfather to Sara's family.

A good funeral is one where we learn about the aspects of a life that were hitherto unknown to us. It took three funerals (in Perth, Melbourne and Ubud) to cover all the aspects of John's life, but they reflect a natural division of his life into three quite distinct parts – each roughly two decades in length, but very different in style and content. The first consisted of his childhood and youth in the rarefied worlds of Geelong Grammar School, the Australian National University (ANU) and Oxford. The second part was his time in Bali where he found his spiritual home and life's work as a filmmaker. The third was back in Australia, as an established filmmaker, but limited by failing health, and sustained by his relationship with Sara. In each part he had family, friends and colleagues, but few of these people span two, let alone three of the parts. This chapter is a brief biographical sketch, divided into those three periods.[1]

Part 1: Rarefied Worlds[2]

Geelong Grammar in the 1940s and 1950s was a world unto itself, as Peronelle Windeyer describes in more detail in the next chapter.

John's father, Sir James Darling, was a significant figure in Melbourne and Australia for reasons that have been documented elsewhere,[3] but throughout the first part of John's life he was headmaster of Geelong Grammar School. He was a larger-than-life figure presiding over the core residential community of the school – the students, staff and their families, all of whom lived on the extensive grounds of the school on the rural fringe of Geelong at Corio. This was a small, enclosed community, dedicated to Darling's progressive vision of education, but separate and somewhat isolated from the city of Geelong and the wider world.

James Darling was generally known as JRD. His political views were more or less socialist and his educational ones progressive and innovative, but his wife was from a conservative Toorak family and socially they were more conservative. The Darlings were the first family of what has been described as a small 'kingdom', and the influence of JRD's persona was pervasive. The first three children were daughters, and a son was long anticipated. When John was born in 1946, there was much rejoicing throughout the school community. Former students have described the occasion in terms usually reserved for royal births.[4]

Consequently John grew up in a position of some privilege, with a surfeit of attention, not to say indulgence, from family and community, but also the mixed blessing and burden of being the son of a 'great man'. Traces of the man he was to become were evident during his schooldays, and have been mentioned by his friends. When the time came for him to follow the expected path to university, he chose not the obvious establishment option of Melbourne University, where his father was a long-standing member of the University Council, but the newer and less conservative ANU. Here his talents for friendship and connection flourished and many friendships from these days continued through his life (see accounts by Ace Bourke and James Darling). He graduated in 1970 with a BA (Hons) majoring in History. He then began a Master of Arts degree at Oxford University, but before it was completed he had been seduced by Bali. The story of this seduction has been told too many times to need repeating here and is related in John's own words in an earlier chapter.

Part 2: Bali

John settled in Bali in 1970, although accounts differ about exactly when. At first he stayed at Kuta Beach. There were few foreigners living in Bali at that time,[5] and most of them were in Sanur or Ubud rather than Kuta, which was little more than a fishing village of simple bamboo houses, just being discovered by a few Australian surfers and aficionados of magic mushrooms.[6] After a few months he moved to Ubud, and soon afterward he had the meeting with Gusti Nyoman Lempad which was to determine the course of his life for the next two decades. This too has become the stuff of legend, but John's own version can be read in his Lempad of Bali essay.

John set up house in a simple *pondok* in the rice fields just uphill of the *banjar* (neighbourhood) of Taman Klod, on what was then the edge of Ubud. This was his home for the next decade and it became a key site in the expatriate scene of the 1970s and 1980s, much celebrated in the memories and memoirs of its veterans.

There were a few other foreigners living in Ubud by this time and more followed through the 1970s. Most were young, and while a few were businesspeople for whom Bali was a convenient and comfortable base, many were artists of one kind or another, students of dance or language, or academic researchers; others were simply immersing themselves in a culture that seemed to make more sense than their own. One who arrived at around the same time as John was Ian van Wieringen, a Dutch-Australian artist whose family had long-standing connections with Indonesia.[7] In 1973 an escaped architecture student from Sydney jumped ship off the coast of Sanur and (according to his self-mythology)[8] swam ashore, was taken in by a local priestly family and never left. His name was Michael White but it soon became Made Wijaya. Van and Made became two of John's closest friends, embarking on adventures in excesses of various kinds and following temple ceremonies across the island.[9]

Other well-known members of the Ubud expatriate community of the time included Linda Garland (designer/entrepreneur of bamboo furniture); Victor Mason (restauranteur, raconteur, Hash House Harrier and birdwatcher); Walter Folle (graphic designer, publisher); John Hardy and Cody and Lyn Shwaiko (designers and exporters of jewellery), as well as longer-established painters such as Han Snel, Arie Smit[10] and the eccentric Antonio Blanco. This community was in some respects similar to, and to a degree styled itself on, the brief golden age of the 1930s, when Walter Spies (polymath artist, musician, ethnographer), Colin McPhee (ethnomusicologist), Jane Belo (anthropologist), and Beryl de Zoete (researcher, critic and performer of dance) lived in Ubud. Some, like the anthropologists Margaret Mead and Gregory Bateson, stayed for shorter periods while others, including celebrities such as Noel Coward, Barbara Hutton and Charlie Chaplin, visited briefly. They were cosmopolitan in outlook but deeply respectful of Balinese culture and committed to intensive study of all aspects of it, beginning with local languages.[11]

The 1970s expatriate scene was in some ways similar, and in one way even more immersive in that, at least initially, expats mostly lived with Balinese families in their own households – a model that became the basis of the homestay accommodation that blossomed in Ubud over the next decade. These expats were regarded by locals with a mixture of the respect due to guests and a bemused tolerance of their eccentricities; but a minority, mostly young men of their own age, were more interested in getting to know them, exchange ideas and knowledge and possibly also to gain economically from association with them. From this commonality of interest came a genuine cultural exchange and friendship across cultures.

Michel Picard, now a noted sociologist of tourism and Balinese religion, recalled his initial arrival in Ubud in 1974 – stepping off the afternoon *bemo* (mini-bus) at the crossroads and seeing two young men playing chess under the big banyan tree in front of Ibu Oka's (later famous) warung. One of them was Nyoman Purpa, a local man from a poor family, who would soon become a pioneering entrepreneur in the new tourism economy. The other was the tall, red-haired Australian John Darling.

Two other people at the heart of this intercultural crossroads were I Gusti Made Sumung, picking up from where he left off with the expats of the 1930s, and Rio Helmi, a much younger man of mixed Turkish and Indonesian descent and cosmopolitan upbringing. Gusti Sumung was a mentor to them both, while John became something of a mentor to Rio, who was in turn a kind of Indigenous expatriate.

This was a small community, with a shared focus on immersion (to varying degrees) in Balinese culture, but also with its own internal rituals of mutual visiting, shared projects, friendships made, developed and broken.[12]

John's notebooks, all in the batik-print covered school exercise books used in those days for everything from government records to researchers' notebooks, reveal an intelligent and sensitive young man working out the things young men try to work out – the meaning of life in general and the direction of his own life in particular – but in the specific context of engagement with and learning about/from Bali, both the pleasures of everyday life and its more mystical and magical aspects. The young man who emerges from these writings is a compulsive researcher, observer, documenter, collector – of material from Balinese life around him and also from a steady diet of reading, especially poetry, spiritual wisdom, and academic writings on Bali. But while he records and collects, he is less sure of what to do with it all, how to organise it, let alone how to make sense of it all. His natural sensibility is less an analytical one than an aesthetic or artistic one, which he expresses in poetry, drawing and painting. He has an endless stream of ideas for projects, but he is, by his own admission, better at starting them than bringing them to fruition, let alone finishing them. The notebooks themselves testify to this, with many started for specific purposes, but few filled. These are characteristics that friends and colleagues would recognise throughout his career.

John's urge to collect and document, and his natural talent for ethnographic research, produced an impressive body of material, especially in art and ritual. While he was interested in academic analysis, his ability to do this was limited by lack of training in anthropology and his natural inclination to revert toward artistic/expressive mode than analytic. Nevertheless a steady stream of academic researchers visited his *pondok* in search of his insights and company. They were drawn by

John's reputation for encyclopaedic knowledge of Bali, and his talent for conversation. But John also knew he needed to learn from them. He was aware of his limitations in terms of ethnographic method, but especially in terms of how to organise and analyse the rich material he was collecting. Then Anthony Forge arrived.

Forge was a British anthropologist based at ANU. He arrived in Bali in 1972. He had previously worked in the Sepik area of Papua New Guinea and, like his forerunner Gregory Bateson, moved his focus (for a combination of practical and intellectual reasons) to Bali to begin a new phase of research on Balinese art.[13] Forge made several more visits to Bali over the next decade and appears to have visited John regularly. His journals mention Forge's visits and his advice about research methods, especially what to look for and focus on. Forge was later to help John again during his time in Canberra when he was editing *Lempad of Bali*.

During these years, John's expertise became known and he was asked to advise and consult on various film and book projects. One of the most important was an exhibition of the work of Walter Spies, finally mounted in the Netherlands and Germany in 1980–81 (see Bruce Carpenter's account at the start of Part III). The project was led by Hans Rhodius, a German collector and patron of the arts who had amassed a considerable collection of Spies's work and in 1964 published a large book about Spies.[14] But through the Lempad family, whom Rhodius also knew, John was invited to write an English text for a book accompanying the exhibition.[15] He is described in the preface as a 'poet and historian'. While John was a competent and fluent writer and liked to think of himself as a poet, he actually published few written works.[16] He was to find his medium elsewhere.

In 1978, John's patron and landlord Gusti Nyoman Lempad died, at the reputed age of 116 years and at a calendrically auspicious time said to have been chosen by himself. This was to be the turning point in John's career and what happened next has again taken on a mythological quality. This too is recorded elsewhere, including in John's own words in Part 1, but in short, he was asked by the family to make a film of Lempad's cremation.

While John knew a lot about Lempad and about Bali, he had no experience and little knowledge about filmmaking. Fortunately, however, his friend Lorne Blair, an established filmmaker, was in Bali at the time with his camera and film stock. Over the following months they worked closely with Gusti Sumung to produce the film *Lempad of Bali*. Anthony Forge then arranged a fellowship for John at ANU, which enabled him to work on some of the archival research and editing of the film in Canberra.

Thus began John's first film which was to launch his career as a filmmaker; it was also a finding of his path and medium as an artist. After years of thinking of himself as a poet, John now found himself a filmmaker.

In June 1980, as John was returning to Bali from Surabaya, where *Lempad of Bali* had been awarded at the Asian Film Festival, he stopped in Sanur and met a young American sculptor recently arrived from Europe. She was Diana Gude, soon to become Diana Darling. They lived together at the *pondok* in Taman from 1981 till 1987. This was a period of what might be called high Bali-philia. Diana recounts in an unpublished memoir:

> In 1981 we married, several times. We had a civil ceremony in Bali, then a church ceremony in Melbourne. When we returned

to Bali, we had a Balinese wedding ceremony as well, because we were besotted by Bali.

To us, being in Bali was like being in an altered state. The air itself seemed populated by a teeming sensibility. This was nothing so simplistic as 'God'. It was a particulate world; but 'gods and demons' is not really an adequate description either. The Balinese religion, we saw, was a hands-on affair. It entailed so much work that there was no room for the sanctimonious piousness I found so obnoxious in my own culture […]

Foreigners have always been seduced by the gorgeousness of Balinese culture, and I think much of the spirituality we sense in it is a product of our own aesthetics. […] The other seductive thing was the Balinese themselves. They are gifted comics. And they have a kind of hyper-androgyny, where both men and women seem to have extra amounts of male and female in them, making the women at once more delicate and more brutal, the men softer and fiercer, than us.

There's no question that we exoticized the Balinese. They were so different from us. In those early days, when people still walked everywhere and carried heavy loads on their heads, the Balinese were physically superior beings. They had finer bones and skin than us, better hair, better memories. They seemed to be super-humanly agile and dextrous. And fearless. They would catch snakes in their bare hands, burrow with their hands for bones in an open grave.

The expat scene in Ubud in those days – which encompassed the 'millionaire's row' of Sayan – was quiet and kept early hours. While people in Kuta would party until breakfast time, in Ubud people were home in bed by nine at night. Ubud expats entertained each other for dinner in their own simple homes; there were hardly any restaurants.

Diana Darling recalls that 'the most interesting company was at the *pondok*':

> I remember the network of Bali researchers and how people would appear on the horizon of the rice fields and then arrive all sweaty at the *pondok*. Some were friends dropping in (Made Wijaya, Lorne Blair, David Stuart-Fox), but sometimes they emanated from the network: the gentle Jack Goody, the brash young Adrian Vickers. Barbara Lovric was sent by Jamie Mackie. I remember Fred Eisemann and his wife Margaret coming to lunch. Angela Hobart came by, not sure about Mark. Michel Picard and Jean-Francois Guermonprez and Deborah Dunn and Cristina Formaggia were little flock of friends that moved together. Henk Schulte Nordholt came, I think, and perhaps Hildred Geertz, and probably Carol Warren. David S-F once brought Hedi Hinzler and the musicologist Tilman Sebas, who was concerned with the conversion of *gangsa jongkok* to *gangsa gendung*[17] on gamelan instruments. Hedi and Tilman were delightfully catty about the younger scholars. There was always a lot of discussion about photocopies of hard-to-find texts.[18]
>
> Among the Balinese who came to visit were Mangku Padang Kerta, his nephew Ketut Budiana, and various friends of Gusti Made Sumung, sometimes with an idea to hold a *mabasan* or a wayang out at the *pondok*. Made Pasek Tempo came to one of these and made a great impression on me. Wianta came and so did Nyoman Gunarsa.[19]

Although John was based in Bali throughout this period, he retained his links with Australia, returning, usually accompanied by Diana, for annual visits to his family in Melbourne, as well as for professional reasons to do with his films. This was a very productive and satisfying period of John's life, apparently unmarred by the creative and personal doubts that beset him at times before and after. It was during these years that he was able to do the filming of his major work, *Bali Triptych*, bringing film crews to Bali for several periods of shooting. He also wrote and directed the 'Master of the Shadows' episode in *The Human Face of Indonesia*. However, finding funding for his films was always a struggle and other obstacles were also emerging.

Diana Darling has said that neither she nor John were cut out for marriage and theirs came to an end in 1987. At this time his health problems were making life in Bali more difficult and he was becoming disillusioned by the enormous changes taking place there. Later that year he moved to Sydney, where *Bali Triptych* was in post-production. Diana remained in Bali.

Part 3: Australia

In Sydney John soon found himself somewhat adrift in a culture he had not lived in for nearly two decades. He worked on proposals for several films, but none came to fruition. He did however continue working with footage previously shot in Bali, producing *Bali Hash* in 1989.

In 1990 he moved to Perth to take a position as lecturer in media production at Murdoch University. Here he met the woman who would be his partner for the rest of his life. John and Sara's families had a long and ongoing association, as Sara's father was a student at Geelong Grammar School when John's father was headmaster. Sara was both a qualified nurse and a graduate from Murdoch University where she had studied film. In 1990 they were introduced and began working together on John's film projects, the first of which was *Below the Wind* (1992). They were married in 1999.

During this period John began to develop and articulate his ideas about film and he became a mentor to young filmmakers. His notes from this period are the closest we have to his theory of film.

But even at this stage of his career he still felt 'a bit of a maverick in the system', 'isolated' and an 'outsider'. He hoped to 'make a special sort of film production school for WA with special reference to SE Asian and Indian students [but] the more I sit in meetings, the less likely I can see it happening.'

At the same time, at a personal level he hoped for more 'recognition for the commitment to making films about Indonesia'. At a professional and artistic level he still felt 'restless and unfulfilled' with a 'creative angst'.[20]

But at the same time, other aspects of his life proved more fulfilling. John had lived a peripatetic life, never having children of his own, and never really experiencing ordinary family life – until this period in Perth when he became a devoted step-parent to Sara's children, especially her son Toby.

During this period, despite Sara's care, his health continued to deteriorate steadily until his underlying problem of haemochromatosis was finally diagnosed in 1996. Haemochromatosis is a genetic disorder in which excessive amounts of iron are absorbed from food and build up in organs such as the liver, heart and pancreas. If undetected and untreated, this excess iron causes organ or tissue damage which can become life-threatening. If it is diagnosed and treated early enough, this damage can be prevented. However it is not easily diagnosed, and in John's case this did not happen until serious damage had already been done. The main symptom is extreme tiredness and lethargy, and this is what prevented John from doing any film work. Even his teaching responsibilities at Murdoch stretched his capacity to the limit, requiring periods of sleep during the working day, and he retired in 1996. But at least the diagnosis meant that it could be managed by treatment; that year he was able to travel to the Cook Islands to run a workshop for local filmmakers.

It is difficult to overstate Sara's role in this part of John's life – organising and managing his affairs, and also his health; literally keeping him alive, possible for years longer than he might otherwise have lived.

In 2001 John and Sara moved to Canberra, where John had a position as Visiting Research Fellow at ANU. This enabled him to do the research toward the film he had long wanted to make about Australian history, *Bleaching Australia*. He was also able to work closely with his distributor and producer Andrew Pike of Ronin Films to secure funding toward the film.

In 2002 the terrorist bombing in Bali motivated him, notwithstanding his fragile health, to make one last film: *The Healing of Bali*.

Throughout his travels John felt some pressure of family expectations – especially from his mother – which he tried to meet through regular visits to Melbourne. In 2007, as his mother's health began to fail, John and Sara moved to Melbourne, partly to be closer to her. Here John turned his artistic eye to painting in acrylics, producing a series of striking images based on the Brindabella mountains which they had been able to see from their house in Canberra. Some of these are reproduced (see image nos. 22–23). John's mother died in 2008, and in 2009 John and Sara moved back to Perth, where Sara's children still lived.

With Sara's constant care John's health was stabilised and he was able to work on writing and developing film ideas. The last time I saw him was in July 2011, on my way home from Bali. He was, as always, interested to hear what was happening there and what I was working on. I mentioned an idea I had been toying with – of writing something about the expat scene in Bali in the 1970s. He jumped at the idea and said, 'even better – let's make a film'. He began digging out old photographs and footage, and we agreed to work on it over the months ahead. A few weeks later he was diagnosed with advanced cancer.

He outlived the doctors' predictions and these final weeks were spent in an uncharacteristically steady and focused ordering of his affairs, receiving last visits and messages from his many friends and preparing for his final hours listening to Balinese music.

Notes

1   This chapter is based in my knowledge of John's story, aided by reminiscences of friends and family, and John's own journals and notebooks, to which I had access at his home in Perth.
2   I am grateful to John's sisters Jane Gray, Caroline Shearer, and Liza Sutherland, and her husband Ivan, for a long conversation in 2012, and also to Peronelle Windeyer, whose own account of these years appears as a separate chapter.
3   Michael Collins Persse, *Well-Ordered Liberty: A Portrait of Geelong Grammar School 1855-1995* (Melbourne: Cliffe, 1995); Peter Gronn, *Just as I Am: A Life of JR Darling* (Melbourne: Hardie Grant Publishing, 2017).
4   Anonymous personal communication, 2012.
5   One of the best known was the Australian painter Donald Friend, whose house in Sanur was the early focus of a group of friends who developed a whole new style of boutique hotels. See Diana Darling, *Tandjung Sari: A Magical Door to Bali* (Singapore: Editions Didier Millet, 2012).
6   Phil Jarratt, *Bali: Heaven and Hell* (Melbourne, London Hardie Grant Books, 2014), 255–257.
7   Ian continued living near Ubud until his death in July 2022, as this book was being prepared for publication.
8   Made Wijaya, *Majapahit Style*, Volume 1 (Denpasar: Wijaya Words, 2014), back cover.
9   Some of these adventures are celebrated in Made Wijaya's *Stranger in Paradise: The Diary of An Expatriate in Bali, 1979-80* (Denpasar: Wijaya Words, 1995).
10 Garrett Kam, *Poetic Realism: The Art of Arie Smit* (Ubud: Neka Museum, 1990).

11 This period has been well documented, contemporaneously by (among others) Hickman Powell, *The Last Paradise* (Oxford: Oxford University Press 1985); Miguel Covarrubias, *Island of Bali* (New York: Knopf, 1937) and more recently by Adrian Vickers, *Bali: A Paradise Created* (Ringwood: Penguin 1989).
12 This brief flowering of a uniquely cosmopolitan/Balinese community has never been systematically documented, but there are glimpses in Made Wijaya, *Stranger in Paradise*; Phil Jarratt, *Heaven and Hell*; Diana Darling, 'Those Were the Days: Bali in the 1980s', *The Yak Online* 69, 12 August 2020.
13 Siobhan Campbell, 'Anthony Forge in Bali: The Making of a Museum Collection', *Visual Anthropology* 27, no. 3 (2014), 248–275.
14 Hans Rhodius, *Schoenheit und Reichtum des Lebens: Walter Spies, Maler und Musiker auf Bali 1895–1942* (Den Haag: L.J.C. Boucher,1964).
15 Hans Rhodius and John Darling, *Walter Spies and Balinese Art*, John Stowell, ed. (Zutphen and Amsterdam: Terra and Tropical Museum, 1980).
16 Mention should be made of the first comprehensive guidebook of Bali entitled *The ABC of Bali: A Guide to the Island of Bali*, written and edited by John Darling, commissioned by the Badung Bali Tourist Promotion Board, 1975.
17 This refers to the conversion of how gamelan keys are set. The old style (*gangsa jongkok*) sat on supports, which gave a muted sound; the *gangsa gantung* were suspended, allowing the keys to vibrate more freely and giving a much bigger, brighter sound. This transformation to what was called *gong kebyar* ('wild gong') started in North Bali and became a craze that swept the island; it remains the standard sound of Balinese gamelan. Only those orchestras too sacred to convert escaped this, and they became very rare; thus their interest to ethnomusicologists.
18 This list reads like a who's who of international researchers in Bali at the time. David Stuart-Fox is an Australian who wrote the definitive book on one of Bali's major temples (*Pura Besakih. Temple, Religion and Society in Bali*, Leiden, KITLV, 2002); he later became librarian at KITLV in Leiden, and more recently published a book on the (in)famous *balian* Ketut Liyer. See David Stuart-Fox and Ketut Liyer, *Ketut Liyer: Pray, Magic, Heal: The Story of Bali's Famous Eat, Pray, Love Folk Healer*, Charles Levine, ed. (New York and Leiderdorp: New Saraswati Press, 2015.) Adrian Vickers is an Australian historian now Professor of Southeast Asian Studies at the University of Sydney. Jack Goody was a prominent British anthropologist who visited Bali briefly. James Mackie was an Australian political scientist specialising in Indonesia. Barbara Lovric was a brilliant Australian researcher on disease, magic and medicine who tragically died young. Fred Eisemann was a self-taught American expert on Balinese culture, author of the perennial two-volume *Bali: Sekala and Niskala*,

1985). Angela Hobart is a German/British anthropologist specialising in ritual. Michel Picard and Jean-Francois Guermonprez are French sociologist/anthropologists. Henk Schulte-Nordholt is a Dutch historian who was for many years head of KITLV. Hildred Geertz is an American anthropologist who did extensive research in Bali from the 1960s until around 2000 and is Emeritus Professor of Anthropology at Princeton University. Carol Warren is an Australian anthropologist working at Murdoch University. Hedi Hinzler is (retired) Professor of Southeast Asian Studies at Leiden University.

19 *Mabasan* is a ritual reading and interpretation of sacred texts. Made Pasek Tempo was a famous dancer. Made Wianta and Nyoman Gunarsa are well-known artists.

20 Quoted from John's notebooks.

1. John as a boy. (John Darling collection)
2. John as a teenager. (John Darling collection)
3. The poet in his in *pondok*, 1979. (Rio Helmi)
4. John in an elegant vintage-style *udeng*. (Made Wijaya)
5. *Pondok* Taman Sari, c.1977. (Made Wijaya)

6. John and Gusti Made Sumung filming *Lempad of Bali*, 1978. (Rio Helmi)
7. Lorne Blair and John filming *Lempad of Bali*, 1978. (Rio Helmi)
8. Lempad at home. (John Darling)
9. Lempad at work. (John Darling)
10. *Rare Angon and the Birth of Kala I*, Lempad's drawing of Rare Angon (Shiva in disguise), his wife, and the demon Kala on which Darling comments in *Lempad of Bali* (Darling 1980). This image is reproduced from Bruce Carpenter et al., *Lempad of Bali: The Illuminating Line* (Ubud, Museum Puri Lukisan, 2016, p. 145). Note that the image in John's film and that published in Carpenter's book are reverses of each other.
11. Lempad's last work, a mask of a new soul to be reborn. (John Darling)

12. John having a cigarette break – probably overlooking the forested gorge immediately east of his *pondok*, 1970s. (Photographer unknown).
13. John in an *ikat* jacket – likely the one referred to by Made Wijaya. (Made Wijaya)
14. Sama Bajo with the DVD of *Below the Wind*, c.1993. (Duncan Graham)
15. John and Haji Bambang meet after thirty years at the site of the Kuta bombing, 2002. (Sara Darling)
16. John's close friend Gusti Puti Purna with a photo John took of his father, Gusti Lingsir Balian. (Graeme MacRae)
17. John and his dog Monty. (Graeme MacRae)

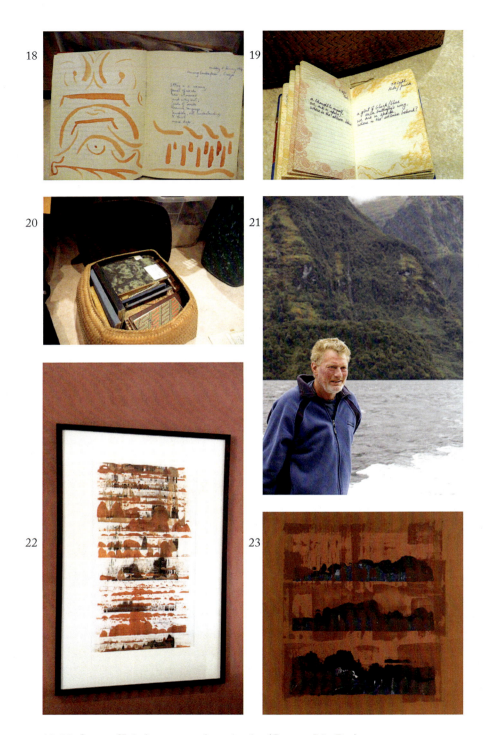

18–20. Some of John's poetry and notebooks. (Graeme MacRae)
21. John at Milford Sound, New Zealand, c.2010. (Sara Darling)
22–23. John's paintings of the Brindabella Mountains. (Sara Darling)

John Darling's Early Life

Peronelle Windeyer

Childhood and youth are times of influences and experiences, some to be discarded, some forgotten and others to be recalled, built upon, adapted and expanded. How many of us can look back at our own childhood and early life and recognise the people and events that set us on the path of our later lives? To do so in relation to others even if we have known them very well carries certain risks. In John Darling's case I can only describe people and events in his life, and leave readers to surmise. John himself acknowledged some such influences.

John always spoke about the community in which he lived his early life as a very special one. In later life he recognised there were echoes of that community, or perhaps even similarities, in the life he led in a village in Ubud in Bali. So what was it about this community that made it a special experience to John and many other children? Is it possible to identify why it was so important in John's early life? Probably not, however, having been a member of that community when John was young, I can provide some background to his life and a description of the community and the life of the children within it.

John's father was Headmaster of Geelong Grammar School and his family was resident at the school. Geelong Grammar is situated at

Corio several miles out of Geelong, which is the second city of Victoria, 47 miles (75kms) southwest of Melbourne. Corio when I was young consisted of little more than a railway station, a Post Office General Store and the school a mile (1.6kms) away. As a result, the population of Corio at that time was largely made up of those employed by and resident at the school and their families. The members of this school community usually referred to themselves as 'Corians'.

John's father, usually referred to as JRD, was born in Tonbridge England to a schoolmaster who ran a 'not very prosperous' preparatory school (JRD Recollections). In his book about the family, JRD's nephew Morris le Fleming said, 'Brought up by a frugal father and a religious Scottish mother JRD and his siblings were inculcated with a strong sense of right and wrong and duty and service'.[1] He continued his education at Repton where the headmaster was William Temple followed by Geoffrey Fisher, both of whom became Archbishops of Canterbury, and then at Oriel College Oxford. Darling was appointed headmaster of Geelong Grammar in 1930, a position that brought more status than wealth. He met his wife Margaret in 1934 on a return voyage after 'home' leave in England. At the time of their marriage she was 20 and he 36. It was to be a long and wonderfully happy marriage.

John, who was born just after the Second World War, was the fourth child and only boy in the family. He was five years younger than the youngest of his three sisters and ten years younger than the eldest. At the time of his birth, John's father had been headmaster for sixteen years and in that time the school had grown in reputation and his father was beginning to be active in education roles outside the school. These increased during the 1950s and, as meetings were often held in Melbourne, he would frequently be away from home when John was still young.

When he was two, John's parents took him and his sister Caroline on a visit to his Darling relations in England while his two eldest sisters remained at boarding school under the care of their maternal grandmother. With them on that trip was a children's nurse who later became a fixture in the Darling household. Nurse Gammon, known as 'Nursey', became much more than a children's nurse and was loved by all the family. She was a particularly important figure in John's life because she was the constant and loving presence in his young life when his parents were increasingly occupied with various official functions associated with his father's public positions and his three sisters were away at boarding school. And John loved her dearly.

The baby of the family, John was the adored little brother of his three sisters. However his birth meant that his immediately elder sister, five years his senior, was displaced as the baby of the family and may have had mixed feelings about her new baby brother! Of course, as John grew beyond babyhood he was sometimes considered a nuisance by his more mature sisters and their friends and there would be an appeal to the adults 'to take Johnny away!' but most of the time his sisters were away at school. He would have been like an only child during school terms and I suspect that John's identification with, and affection for, the local Corio/Geelong Grammar community was generated at that time because there were always other children around and the families of those children were always welcoming.

John's formal schooling began at Bostock House, a Geelong Grammar primary school in Geelong, and continued at the boarding Junior School at Corio for his upper primary and early secondary years. Like other sons of teaching staff, John was a full member of a boarding house, but it was 'board' without 'lodging': he slept at home. (That exception was presumably to ensure that staff sons did not occupy the beds that could be used by full fee paying students.)

The situation in which the headmaster's son is a student at the school would raise questions about how it would work for John in his relations with other boys, and perhaps even for staff. There are reasons why it did work for as long as it was necessary. The Junior School was administratively far enough removed for John to have no contact with his father. However, on entering the Senior School there was the potential for father and son to meet. JRD timed his retirement with this in mind. In his book *Richly Rewarding* he says, 'Our son John was reaching a position in the school in which it would be no longer possible for us to disregard each other … and he would have a better chance under a new headmaster'.[2] There must have been some interesting discussions in the family about how they would 'disregard' each other at school.

John was not unique in being the son of a member of staff and a boarder sleeping at home. In John's case there were several sons of staff in his House, two of whom were also in his year, and of course he moved into the Senior School with established friendships from Junior School. At that time the first year in the Senior School was Year 9, and schooling for Year 10 was at Timbertop, the school's country campus in the mountains. It was while John was at Timbertop that his father retired, leaving him to finish his senior years without the potential for complications arising from his relationship with the headmaster.

While he was at school John suffered periods of undiagnosed illness which presumably related to the genetic condition which so badly damaged his body over the many years before it was eventually diagnosed when he was 50. Between these bouts of illness he had the stamina to be a good long-distance and cross-country runner at school. He was a keen cricketer and a member of the First Xl. He loved cricket and followed the Australian Test Series but perhaps an even greater love was the Geelong AFL football team.

John Darling's experience of growing up in the Geelong Grammar (or Corio) community was something that he valued all his life. For adults in the community its value was both social and professional, for the children it was something special. John's father recognised this special quality too. At a gathering late in his life he told a group of us that we should be writing about what it was like to be 'the children of Corio' when we were young. It was a time when there were fewer staff and the school was still fairly isolated from Geelong itself both of which factors contributed to the creation of a close knit community: one in which families helped and often depended on each other. Although there was a professional hierarchy amongst teaching staff, there was no social hierarchy among the families, especially none among their children. Looking back it seemed to have been a magical time for children.

For children, Geelong Grammar was their playground during school holidays. There were all the outdoor facilities such as tennis courts, a tennis-practice wall, a swimming pool and plenty of space. The double rows of cypress trees that formed windbreaks around the school provided wonderful tree-climbing opportunities in which children could start on one tree and transfer to the next all above the ground. The longest transfers were across five or six trees and it was usually with a multi-aged group of children in which the older and more experienced climbers helped and encouraged the timid and younger ones. The school quad and the smooth bit of school road just inside the green school gates were wonderful places for roller-skating although some staff members were not happy when they met young roller skaters in the quad, even though it was during school holidays. The extensive grounds provided vast and safe spaces for bicycle riding and games of 'bicycle chasey', usually in small groups of similar aged children. Bicycles also gave us access to the local store and sweet shop a mile away.

For children, much of the charm of this environment seemed to be in the closeness of friendships among both children and their parents, which generated a very relaxed 'open house' approach. It was like belonging to more than one family and John, with or without one of his sisters, joined my family for picnics and outings and even on occasions for short camping type holidays.

The friendliness of the community was fostered in part through the Community Centre, which had been built by the school for the community of staff. The Centre provided two grass tennis courts, a children's playground, and a multi-use building that among other uses, housed the Nursery School which was staffed by a qualified kindergarten teacher. That the outdoor areas of this facility were maintained by the people of the community was an expression of, and contributed to, the co-operative spirit of those years.

John's experience of the warmth and close friendships that existed at Corio would presumably have contributed to his appreciation of being part of the community in a traditional village such as the one he belonged to so many years later in Bali.

While community and shared families were important in John's childhood, the major influence on his young life was that of his parents. JRD preached the values of honesty and integrity, a concern for people and a sense of responsibility towards others, particularly those who were less privileged – and he practiced what he preached. To what extent John embraced or accepted, adopted and adapted, or ignored those values is made clear throughout this book. However, it is important to note that John as a child, young man and as a pupil in his father's school would have been totally conscious of what his father stood for.

He would have heard it on occasions such as the sermons his father preached in the chapel and he would have seen it in practice in the way his father related to people and the community and in the many organisations which his father chose to support.

While John enjoyed a strong bond with his father through common interests in history, in literature, in ideas and ethics, and in intellectual discussions, he was always very close to his mother. His creativity and sensitivity to beauty in language, in art, in the environment and in personalities were demonstrated not only in his films but also in his poetry and painting.

John's spirituality could be described as free ranging, perhaps even wide ranging. It was not limited by the strong Anglican tradition of his parents' faith but incorporated elements of Christianity with those of other faiths, particularly Buddhism. It exemplified adoption and adaptation. This was beautifully demonstrated in his funeral service, which he planned and designed during his final illness. The service included an Aboriginal smoking ceremony and traditional Balinese Hindu-Buddhist rites within a Christian service.

There will always be certain expectations placed on the only son in a family, even if such expectations are never expressed. As he grew up, John would have become aware that this was so. While his path in life may have been different from anything his parents might have envisaged, I am certain that they were never disappointed in him, indeed they were proud of who he became.

Note

1 Morris le Flemming, *The Darlings of Eyke and the Nimmos of Falkirk*, privately published, England, 2007.
2 Sir James Darling, *Richly Rewarding: An Autobiography*, Melbourne: Hill of Content Publishing, 1978, 206.

John Darling, Old Ubudian

Diana Darling

The first conversation I ever had with John Darling was in June 1980 in the parking lot of the Bali Oberoi. It went like this:

'Are you Made Wijaya?' I said.

'No.'

My friends and I were to be introduced to John and Made at dinner that evening. It was easy enough to confuse the two: we had been told that they were both Australian, both redheads, and that they knew as much about Bali as any foreigners since Walter Spies.

Later John opened up considerably, and he told me about how he first came to Bali. He had been at Oxford studying for a doctoral degree in history when, some time around 1970, he met an adventurous American girl who persuaded him to drop out and go to Indonesia with her. They sailed around the archipelago and ended up living in a bamboo hut near Ubud. But after a while she went on to do other things, and he was left alone with his books, his handwritten poems and a broken heart.

One night he was feeling particularly lonely and he went wandering, as one still may do, through the rice fields in the moonlight. I can see him so easily – a tall, lanky, rose-coloured man in batik pyjamas, with his long nose sniffing the warm night air. John says that while he was wandering around worrying about love, picking his way over the criss-crossing of dykes and the rushing of water through the fields, through clouds of fireflies and under a rolling night sky, he came across a tiny, bright-eyed and very old man wrapped in a blanket, sitting by an irrigation ditch and smiling at him.

John says that when he saw the old man he was so happy to see another human being that he just sat down beside him. They tried to converse, but the old man didn't speak Indonesian and John didn't speak Balinese. So John offered him a clove cigarette, and they sat there together in the dark and brilliant world of the rice fields, the young man and the old man, looking out at the night. The moon was three-quarters full, bright enough for them to see each other well. John didn't know it at the time, but he was sitting with the venerable artist, I Gusti Nyoman Lempad.

Some time after this, John went to watch a *wayang kulit* performance at the Lempad house. After the performance, a slim elderly man came up to him and said, 'Excuse me, but my father has noticed you and he has said that you should come and live on our land.'

This was Lempad's son, I Gusti Made Sumung. John accepted the offer, and eventually he built a little *pondok*, or farmer's cottage, out at the edge of the rice fields overlooking a rather spooky river gorge.

Gusti Made Sumung had plenty of sons of his own, but none of them listened to his ideas and opinions with the same deferential attention as John did, and the two men became very close. When Lempad died several years later at the age of 116, John went to the family house, as was customary, and found the courtyard full of people busy preparing for the funerary rituals. John apologised to Gusti Made Sumung.

'I'm sorry, I don't know what I can do to help', he said. 'I'm not very good with a meat cleaver.'

He answered, 'Make a film of my father's cremation'.

Later Gusti Made Sumung recounted, 'I must have been in trance when I said that. I don't know where the idea came from. I knew John was a poet, not a filmmaker.' But John's friend Lorne Blair had just returned to Bali from shooting a segment with his brother Lawrence of their *Ring of Fire* series, and he had a camera and some film. With Gusti Made Sumung's guidance, they shot Lempad's cremation and the preparations leading up to it. Then they decided to expand the project and document Lempad's long life as well, giving John a chance to apply some of his prestigious education as a historian. The film *Lempad of Bali* became a classic in the filmography of Bali, and John had discovered in filmmaking a way to make his poetry visible.

In the films that he went on to make – especially in his major work, the three-part series *Bali Triptych* – John seemed to be searching for a way to show others what it was about Bali that moved him so. He regarded Bali with something close to reverence, and observed its uniquely elaborate customs with a rigour that was almost courtly. No important undertaking should begin without consulting the Balinese calendar, no opportunity missed to celebrate an obscure Balinese holy day with offerings and perhaps a reading of Balinese poetry. His friends were mostly foreign scholars of Bali and old Balinese literati. His library at the *pondok* was formidable, much of it carefully collected photocopies of scholarly articles and monographs. He spoke high Balinese rather haltingly, with a patrician Australian accent.

John's determination to make films led him to move back to his native Australia in 1987. The neolithic level of technology at his *pondok* obliged it, since there was no electricity there, and no telecommunications.

Over the next 20-odd years he made a number of documentaries on Bali and other societies in Indonesia; and for many years he taught filmmaking at Murdoch University in Perth, despite being constrained by a rare and debilitating blood disease. In all this he was greatly helped by his second wife, Sara, whom he married in Australia in 1999 on 13 November, a date he selected as auspicious according to the Balinese calendar. His last film was *The Healing of Bali* (2003), about the 2002 Bali bombings and launched on their first anniversary. It was a project he described, somewhat grandly, with the word *karya*, the Balinese term for ritual or holy work.

In October 2011, John was diagnosed with untreatable cancer and given a shockingly short prognosis: 'weeks, possibly days'. He prepared for his death with grace and good humour, and uncharacteristic efficiency. He planned the details of his funeral. His books and papers will go to the National Library in the collection 'Australians in Asia'. He took care to communicate with his friends. He was grateful when two of them – Made Wijaya and Jero Asri Kerthyasa – visited him in Perth and brought him holy water from Bali, of the particular sort required for the release of the soul. A week before he died he sent an SMS to Made Wijaya saying that, since it was Hari Raya Saraswati (the Balinese day to honour the deity of knowledge and the arts), he was spending the day cleaning his books. He spent the last day of his life listening to recordings of Balinese music that he had chosen weeks earlier and labelled 'John's last listening'. To all who bade him good-bye, his last words were 'I love you'.

Originally published in The Bud, *Bali, January 2012.*

My Favourite Redhead

Made Wijaya

I first met John Darling in 1976 at a posh all-men's tennis afternoon in Killara, a fashionable garden suburb of Sydney. Our mutual friend Ace Bourke had orchestrated the meeting and, despite the friction that often existed between fellow redheads and homosexualists in Australia in those days (eyeing each other off across playgrounds and such), we became instant doubles partners. He was a terrible cheat and a poor loser but he had an immaculate backhand. In fact, in the decades of close friendship that followed, Johnny was always describing elegant cricket strokes in the air whenever he felt particularly chuffed – such as after he'd over-tipped the delivery man bringing Captagon-brand amphetamines, or while he was getting dressed for a date with a rich hippy girl with big tits.

The obituaries about Johnny have been correct, but they omitted, out of courtesy I imagine, to mention what a narcissist Johnny was – but in a nice, not a nasty way. Under all that aesthete and ascetic lurked a giant ego, and a fairly healthy disregard for other people's time and whiskey. He was a natty dresser too – favouring the grey shoes of his academic upbringing teamed with a plaited belt to exaggerate his snake hips. I don't think I ever saw him in a short-sleeved shirt. In 1985 Australian actress Arna-Maria Winchester made him the first Sawu-blanket jacket with coconut shell buttons which I bet he wore in hospital on his death bed whilst listening to the gamelan music he loved so much (see image no. 13).

In the early 1980s I visited Johnny's exquisitely Middle Earth '*Pondok* Plus' every Sunday morning: he was the only person I knew with bread, Blue Band margarine and Vegemite. He would while the day away gardening and listening to the cricket on his transistor radio while I would lie, seductively, on some hessian pillows, waiting for Rio to turn up. Even today, almost 35 years later, there are still women at the Yoga Barn doing the same thing!

In the late 1980s, Johnny and Ian Van Wieringen and I became 'The Three Bli(s)',[1] dedicating our lives to late nights in Legian and Legong. We are celebrated in a famous leg-shot from that era. We were like culture-conscious cat burglars: Van got all the girls, Johnny all the grants and I caught the crabs. Johnny was brilliant at getting grants. He deserved a leg-up: while his business sense was poor, his understanding of the real Bali and his poetic vision were unique.

He was a great mentor to me in all my encore careers since failing to become Wimbledon tennis champion at age 16 – even in my latest incarnation as a barefoot documentary filmmaker – doing just the sort of films Johnny used to make, but in 24 hours and in lower definition. 'It took me twenty years to learn to do that,' he said, 'and you've done a hundred films in three months.'

He was like my Dad in this way, always supportive and kind.

This piece was originally published in Ubud Now & Then, *3 July 2013, formerly available from http://ubudnowandthen.com.*

Note
1   '*Bli*' in Balinese means 'older brother'.

My Friend John Darling

Rio Helmi

A couple of weeks ago I got an email from Australian filmmaker John Darling's widow, Sara, asking me to give an introductory talk to the screening of his (and Lorne Blair's) classic Bali film, *Lempad of Bali*. I had little hesitation in accepting – Johnny was an old and dear friend who in some ways was something of a Bali mentor for me. It was only after I started thinking about it that I realised that this was not really an easy task, to do justice to an extraordinary man who was so much a product of his cultural setting: he grew up the scion of a well-respected Australian family in the 1950s and '60s, yet at the same time was an avid explorer of ideas extremely foreign to his background; a man who was an unwitting exponent of old-fashioned values yet at the same time was very much part of the avant-garde.

In his biography attached to the invitation to the screening of his film, it said that John was educated in Canberra and in Oxford, majoring in history. This is true. But where John was really formed was at home and at Geelong Grammar, Australia's most prestigious school. The two were for him almost inseparable. His father was headmaster there for just over three decades; he was knighted later for his services to education and broadcasting (he was chairman of the ABC for seven years). No matter how much John rebelled (dropping out of university, living in a hut in the rice fields), his respect for his father was ineradicable. John couldn't wait to get himself out of Geelong, but you couldn't take the 'proper cricket' out of John.

The same bio calls him a filmmaker. Again, this is true, but to me Johnny was foremost a gentleman and a poet. When we first met in the mud-walled, dirt-tracked, unelectrified, quiet village that Ubud was in the very early 1970s, John described himself to me as a poet. Spending time with him on expeditions through Bali and at his neat little mud-floored bamboo hut convinced me that he was a real gentleman. I could tell, because I was still in my late teenage rebellion against it and knew gentility when I saw it. But with John it didn't bother me: his was a mind that was open, exploring, searching, daring to fathom new depths. This was no stilted bourgeois academic. This was the real deal.

Johnny tried to be courteous even when he would occasionally lose his redhead temper. I remember that at the height of a heated disagreement with Lorne's brother, Lawrence, over whether the Lempad film should be part of the Blair brothers' *Ring of Fire* series, he struggled to be polite and maintain his sense of fairness. Lawrence had not really been directly involved in the film. However he felt, rightly or wrongly, that as Lorne had been an essential part of it, *Lempad* should be one of the series. John agonised for weeks trying to find a 'correct' – that is, fair – way to solve his dilemma.[1]

John could never have survived in a world of pure academia. It fed the intellectually inquisitive side of his mind, but it didn't fulfil the gentle romantic, the wildly vulnerable heart that was always ready to reach out, that always insisted on trying to be fair to all – the cultural explorer in him that needed to do more than just catalogue and annotate. Johnny needed to live it.

In the bio it says he was fluent in Indonesian and Balinese. I have to say this is only half true. John's spoken Balinese was halting at best and his accent in Indonesian was atrocious, though he did know the languages and the terms.[2] But it was his honesty and evident kindness that made people trust him and allow him in, despite his perceived eccentricity. These qualities opened the doors to the most extraordinary experiences for him around Bali and Indonesia as a whole.

For a few years we shared the same 'landlord', if that is what you could call Gusti Made Sumung, Lempad's son. In reality Gusti Sumung was a complex mix of landlord, uncle, wily fox, and repository of Bali lore, a man whose career included being *sedahan* (a kind of overseer) of the dry fields north of Ubud that were part of the *subak* irrigation system, as well as an assistant to Walter Spies, and a stint as Margaret Mead and Gregory Bateson's secretary/assistant.[3] Gusti Sumung always had something in his hat for us, especially for John who was evidently much more of a willing student than I was, the wild runaway boy from Jakarta. And Gusti Made Sumung knew how to broker win-win deals: John made a film that honoured Gusti Sumung's father Lempad, but that also became the beginning of a whole new career for John, whose love for Bali and its culture was a lifetime affair, a marriage that lasted until death. Towards the very end of his life, I am told, he tidied up and arranged his library and reference books, then took care to have all his favourite Balinese gamelan music tapes digitised. As he lay dying this music was plugged into the speakers of the hospice room, and he passed away surrounded by his wife and family listening to his favourite Balinese ritual music. I wouldn't be surprised to find out that my friend Johnny has been reincarnated somewhere on Bali.

My Friend John Darling

This piece was originally published in Ubud Now & Then, *26 June 2013, formerly available from http://ubudnowandthen.com*

Notes

1. In the end John decided not to include *Lempad of Bali* in the series.
2. In letter to a friend dated 1 June 1977, John wrote 'I'm still keeping up with the Balinese – slow work but my Balinese friends seem to be enjoying my stumbling attempts'. (Sara Darling collection).
3. Gusti Sumung did know Mead and Bateson, but it was their protégée Jane Belo that he worked for.

A Tribute to John

Tjokorda Gde Mahatma Putra Kerthyasa

I met John Darling for the first time when I was a baby – just after I had been born – around the time he was helping the film crew shooting the Eka Dasa Rudra,[1] the most important ceremony held in Bali in living memory.

His major work, *Bali Triptych*, captures the true nature and essence of Bali in a way that few others have done since, in either film or writing. It's an eerie, haunting introduction which brought back some of my earliest coherent memories of Bali, as I sat in a Sydney flat trying to recall the feelings, the sensations and infantile memories of my birthplace.

John was an 'adopted' son of Bali and Ubud, so we bring offerings for him. Those on the coffin are the materials he will need in the afterlife. His friend Madé Wijaya has brought a red lion sarcophagus, a small effigy, to represent what he would have been in Bali. He was loved by the people of Ubud.

In Ubud he was Ketut John – and proud of it – or Johndarling, pronounced as a single name. He was 'adopted' by Gusti Made Sumung, the son of the great artist Gusti Nyoman Lempad, and lived on their land where he made his *pondok*, his farmer's cottage, and worked his land. He told me rice cultivation was, I quote, 'Bloody hard work!' So I have never done it myself. But he understood that this was part of the essence of Balinese life – the peaceful methodical side to balance the frantic rituals.

When John was tending his rice paddy, Ubud was a very different place. The main road was unsealed, he had no electricity but lots of fireflies. He was one of the only outsiders, or *'tamu'* (guests) who truly loved the place for what it was – not just for what they could get out of it. John was a man who lived truth and spoke it. He didn't choose an easy life in Bali, he chose a Balinese life.

He is remembered by the people of Ubud as one of the few foreign 'custodians' of Balinese culture who didn't take it, but shared it. His work I consider to be *'karya'*, great works that will continue to be an important reminder to my generation of what is truly important in Bali, in a time when we see great change – some for the better, some for the worse.

I met John and Sara a few years ago in Berrima between Sydney and Canberra for tea. After talking about footy, cricket and tea, our conversation came back to Bali, as it always did. John implored me to 'learn the old ways'. Visionary that he was, he saw not only the immense change in Bali but the fragile balance that needs to be maintained. And by old ways, I feel he meant more than just the rituals, but as much the old values of the Australian gentleman he was – sportsmanship, helping your mate, telling the truth.

On behalf of the Desa Adat Ubud and my father Tjokorda Raka Kerthyasa, as a friend of John and the Bendesa Adat, or cultural and spiritual custodian of Ubud, we pray for John Darling on the day of his cremation. May his soul find a clear and peaceful journey to its place in the Universe, but remember to pass by Ubud on the way.

Tjokorda Gde, from the Ubud ruling family, spoke at John's funeral in Perth.

Note

1   A huge series of purification rituals held in 1979.

Belonging and Grace

James Darling

Our beloved Johnny was a will-of-the-wisp, otherworldly character who trod lightly on the ground. His thin, angular body contained a resilient, resolute and steadfast spirit. He was also laid back, eccentric, frugal, bookish and academic. He crossed the divides of race and culture with consummate ease and carried an intrinsically Australian love of sport – cricket and the Geelong Football Club in particular – all his days.

Who can forget the boy with flaming red hair, fair skin and freckles, in creams, under a floppy white hat, wearing an oversized sleeveless sweater and lathered in zinc cream as he took the field?

Throughout his life Johnny was inevitably charming, a compulsive storyteller with an impish, ironic and self-deprecating humour.

It was no surprise that he gravitated to Asia, to Bali and its all-encompassing metaphysics, its exquisite beauty, its quietude and passivity, its forbearance.

Bali became integral to the effort to find and to express himself, which was not easy, not without critical anxiety and self-doubt – the last born and only son in whom much was invested, and which he struggled to reply to, let alone repay, as if in defiance of the family he loved instinctively and inevitably, with the fear of not belonging, which could undermine moral purpose and dovetail back to a self he found wanting.

He journeyed with the pace of a wanderer.

It is also a fact of Johnny's life that he was ridiculously irresistible to women who tried to mind him, improve him, love him, and care for him.

For more than 20 years it has been Sara whose common sense and practicality anchored him and literally extended his life. Sara brought the gift of the affection of her growing family, gave John a sense of fatherhood and, more recently, the role of grandfather to children whom he adored and who loved him unreservedly.

I heard about Johnny before I met him. It was an indelible moment. I was an 11-year-old in a dormitory waiting for lights out on my first night at boarding school: it was Barwon House, Geelong Grammar, and the headmaster came and sat on my bed. JRD, as I grew to know him, spoke about the First XI and winning the premiership. 'You and my boy Johnny,' he growled. It was an admonition, a command, a voice like the clashing of rocks over gravel.

And while we were in the First XI and missed playing the final by one run, the prophesy linking John and me through cricket spanned more than five decades to our poignantly unforgettable, last, long-distance conversation as he was watching the second Test between Australia and South Africa on Fox Sports. 'I have just a small window before tiredness', he said, 'and I wanted to talk with you'. He told me he had just finished *In the Light of Eternity*. 'And I have been reading my father's writings', he said. I have never had such an awareness of a lifelong friendship and a final conversation.

The front page for the 'Thanksgiving for the life of John Austin Campbell Darling' has a photo of Johnny in a blue tracksuit top and matching T-shirt in front of a wide rushing river with steep bush as background. There is that quizzical, astute, penetrating and inviting gaze. Turn the page and there are the words: 'In the last weeks of his life John applied the same processes he used to produce his films. He planned, created and visualised his entire funeral. Here then is his final work.'

Johnny was inevitably modest. He was quietly joyous in the knowledge that he could do what others might never expect and could surprise even himself. I saw *Below the Wind*, turning on the ABC completely by chance, and was immediately captivated. Even missing the titles, I knew it had to be John's work. Who else could engender the necessary trust and respect to explore the disparate cultures and connections between Aboriginal Australia and the Indonesian archipelago before white settlement? Characteristically, *Below the Wind* broke new ground. It was poetic, astute, informative and original.

Fittingly, John's thanksgiving service was an evocative and seamless cross-cultural celebration involving Indigenous Australia, Christianity and Balinese Hindu traditions. It began with a smoking ceremony conducted by an Aboriginal priest, Rev. Sealin Garlett, who welcomed Johnny's spirit, honoured among his people, to take its place and to reside in his country. The service interwove the great poetic aspirations of Christian spirituality with the journey, affinity and repose of Balinese Hindu tradition. Choked with emotion and through unrestrainable tears, the prince Tjok Gde (Tjokorda Gde Mahatma Putra Kerthyasa) from Ubud spoke of Johnny as part of his family, gave an offering and blessing for his soul, and, with prayers for his new journey, sprinkled the flowers of his coffin with flicks of holy water. John chose his long-time friend, Ace Bourke, to give the eulogy. Ace spoke of Johnny's life with comprehensive candour, insight and love. With Ace's permission I would like to borrow the three attributes that Johnny requested that he address in his eulogy: his manners, his humour and his essence.

His manners, Johnny asserted, came from his mother whom he loved deeply and irrevocably. Of course he was right, but I would go further. Manners were his means of connection. It was a family trait, instilled with the love of his elder sisters, exhorted into fruition by his father and nurtured by his mother. He was a gentle man whose ability to carry himself simply and clearly cut through barriers, crossed boundaries, and inspired trust and unreserved affection.

John's humour was subtle, sardonic, rapier-sharp and full of self-deprecation. He invited you to laugh at absurdity, at self-importance, at the pompous or the illogical. His take on the world was akin to a poke in the ribs. Humour informed his judgement, his sense of social justice, his passion about what was real and what was not.

Essence begins at the beginning, what was always there. Winning the marathon at Timbertop, Johnny exhibited stamina and resilience, mental toughness and physical endurance. He was focused, competitive and able to deal with pain to achieve a goal. Essence could be in the elegance of a cover drive, or, just as readily, it could be found in adversity and the relationships you form in the furnace of troubles. Essence may be revealed in art, in film, through an enduring family or by the accidents of chance. Essence can be shaped, as Johnny was, by a debilitating condition that was undiagnosed for most of his life.

Johnny's fear of perpetual wandering, the restlessness of not belonging, paradoxically belied the fact that he belonged, and was welcomed, wherever he went.

Today we say our goodbyes, rich in the knowledge that 'he loved us' – to borrow Ace's words – 'as much and as easily as we loved him'.

In that poignant last phone call Johnny told me that he faced his death more easily than he had faced much of his life. It was an extraordinary preparation for his inevitable departure: organised, inclusive, and mindful of others, especially Sara.

From the deep roots of family and with the affinity of his many friends, with integrity and with eloquence, Johnny expressed the grace and ordinariness of living. His spirit partook of grace.

This tribute was given on 19 December 2011 at St George's Church, Malvern, Victoria. (James and Johnny are not related.)

A Eulogy for John Darling

Ace Bourke

I arrived in Perth soon after hearing of Johnny's grave diagnosis. Although he had been unwell for years, it was still a shock. For someone so ill, he looked fine, had surprising stamina, was very clear and lucid, and was as sweet and welcoming as ever. Sara, with help from her daughter Danielle, was looking after him 24/7, and there was a relay of people through the house – palliative nurses, lawyers, a masseuse, household helpers and, of course, the gorgeous grandchildren.

One of the first things Johnny said to me was, 'Not seeing them grow up is my saddest regret'.

The telephone kept ringing, and emails kept coming from around the world – many from friends, old girlfriends, film fans, academics, students, and Baliophiles.

Despite all this activity, Johnny, the eye of the storm, was quietly reading *The Australian* newspaper in what was obviously his favourite position on the sofa and drinking endless cups of coffee or Diet Coke. Monty the dog, however, looked depressed.

He had been given only two weeks to live, but survived for eight, giving him time to get everything organised, which he did with quiet determination. I think he felt that Sara, whom he loved deeply, was now securely set up in an attractive house with the supportive family of Danielle and Mark and their three young children nearby.

Those extra days and weeks were precious and Johnny showed us how to face death and the end of life. Not only did he manage to make this time a pleasure to be with him, but he left us with directions, instructions and advice for the future.

Prone to procrastination, he was now, despite the illness, incredibly focused and resolute, with superhuman stamina for several projects.

There was to be a Lempad exhibition at the Puri Lukisan Museum in Ubud in August 2013. Chris Hill, whom Johnny had met at Murdoch University, was working on an accompanying publication with Sara, which included Johnny's memoir of Lempad and some of his photographs and poetry. He was happy to hand over the boxes with relevant material to Chris and see them taken away.[1]

On the Sunday before he died, Johnny worked late into the night going through the last box of material on Lempad to be sorted, identifying photographs, etc., and leaving comments and instructions. In the morning he explained everything to Sara. He collapsed at 11am and was taken to hospital. On the Thursday as he was being transferred to a hospice, he said to Sara, 'In my head I'm already in Bali'. He died on the Saturday night.

Living in Bali for 20 years was the centre of Johnny's life. Living in a simple dwelling (*pondok*) in the rice fields of Ubud, his albino cow one of his few possessions, he seemed to find his spiritual home and life's work. As predicted by Manning Clark, who lectured us both at ANU, and recently affirmed by Melbourne University historian Charles Coppel in an email, 'John Darling's contribution to the Australian understanding of Indonesia was unique'.

Johnny also wanted to publish his poetry in a book that initially he thought may include some of his father's poems. He specifically wanted my help with this. Luckily Lucinda, Sara's sister, came to Perth after I had left and worked very hard with Johnny on this, reading much of the poetry aloud. Johnny, with extraordinary stamina, described the context of the poems, made some minor revisions, alterations and additions that he never imagined he would get around to doing.

The other unresolved project was his paintings going back to his Canberra days in the early 2000s. I'd seen some of them before but had no idea there were so many, and that he had such ability. He was influenced by the Brindabella Mountains which was the view from their house, but in addition to a good sense of composition and colour, he was inspired by the textures and tones of the actual ochres that he collected and ground up to use. The paintings moved between figurative and abstract, and some successful work that was very calligraphic. Again with amazing stamina, we went through and sorted all his paintings while he talked to me about them: what he was trying to achieve, and if he felt he had succeeded. He was also a good photographer, and his love of nature is manifest in both his photographs and in his paintings.

Johnny had apparently said that in his eulogy he wanted three things acknowledged: the good manners his mother had taught him – OK, let's acknowledge he had great manners. He also thought his sense of humour was misunderstood – so luckily, shortly after John's death, his artist friend George Galitzine emailed from London saying Johnny was

> such a lovely, sweet man, who always had a great understanding of the idiocies and ironies of life, which he would share so hilariously with everyone. I recall always laughing a lot with him, as he kept

us all in stitches with his self-deprecating stories and wonderful take on the vagaries of his fate.

And lastly, John wanted who he was – his essence – talked about in his eulogy, not the chronological timeline. I felt he was telling me what he found important about life, our lives, and giving me advice for the future while I was letting him know how I felt about him in case this was my last chance.

He exhibited such courage and patience, good humour, equanimity and quiet determination. As Made Wijaya has noted, he expressed no self-pity, just a concern for those he would be leaving.

He has always been the person I've enjoyed talking to most, as he was a good listener, and he himself spoke amusingly, insightfully and concisely about interesting and quite complex subjects. I think one could say he had a beautiful mind.

He told me he didn't want to be a wandering spirit, he wanted to belong here. If possible he wanted the appropriate protocols to be carried out by the Aboriginal people – in the same way that the appropriate Balinese customs are being followed – at his funeral. He was very concerned about ongoing Aboriginal dispossession and disadvantage – and the slow pace of reconciliation.

Johnny and I met at ANU both doing Arts degrees and got on easily right from the start. We had had similar interests and education – Johnny had attended Geelong Grammar, where his father was headmaster. We both have colonial ancestors, lovely families, marvellous parents and great sisters; Johnny was the youngest child, with Jane, Liza and Caroline ahead of him. Understandably, he may have been a little spoilt. We discussed how our families gave us the confidence to lead our own lives, even if our parents didn't entirely understand the direction. He was very close to his mother and was a surprisingly shrewd financial investor for them both. Although she died three years ago, he still missed her very much.

No matter where Johnny was, he was always able to get international news, books to read, and to be able to listen to the cricket and football. In fact he was a news junkie – he listened to the news all day and into the night, liked ABC Radio National, read the newspapers, loved the New York Review of Books, and various internet sites.

We were both born in 1946. When I turned sixty-five he said, 'I don't think being 65 is looking like a great year for me – but, unlike you, at least I'll escape travelling around giving talks to Probus'.[2] He wished he would have lived to 75.

While I never visited him in Bali, our lives criss-crossed. He was at Oxford University while I was in London, and we hitchhiked through Spain with him lugging his books. He was in Sydney when I opened my first gallery, and he suggested several artists. And he lived with me in Sydney when he was editing *Lempad of Bali*. When he was working on the documentary *Bleaching Australia*, about mostly unreported massacres of Aboriginal people, our working lives overlapped.[3]

Johnny and I never particularly discussed our religious beliefs, but he said he certainly leant more towards Eastern religions like Buddhism and Balinese Hinduism. I did cheekily ask, 'what do you think happens to us when we die' and got a rather annoyed: 'I don't know!' He said he could face his judgement – if that is what happens – as he had tried to lead a useful and beneficial life, and had 'never consciously hurt anyone'. He was not a conflicted person ever really – and now I was in awe of his maturity and calmness. He was at peace with himself.

In his last weeks he paced himself to make (or take) all the telephone calls he thought were necessary. Some of these calls were with ex-girlfriends. He was a romantic, and was attractive in an unusual way and always very popular. After his diagnosis he skyped his first wife Diana Darling, and spoke to both ex-girlfriends, Nicola Flamer Caldera in Sydney and Margaret Burrell in Adelaide, whom I also knew well from ANU and who was due to visit. They were still very fond of him and he was of them. While Johnny enjoyed various aspects of Oxford University, and flat mates like Christopher Hitchens, his heart was probably not in his thesis on 'Concepts of Empire'. It was another girlfriend who encouraged him to take a break and travel to Asia and Indonesia, where Johnny instantly felt at home.

But he spent his last 21 years extremely happy with Sara, and I think we all have to thank her for looking after him so well and actually giving him a few extra years. They were a great team, and they worked on the various projects that Johnny could manage together. Sara also came with two children, Danielle and Toby, to whom Johnny was a much-loved father, and in the last few years, an adored and adoring grandfather to their children.

At the dinner with Johnny's sister in Perth before he died, I first heard about Nursey who came to the family at Corio as a nanny soon after Johnny was born. I think he rather liked having a 'nursey' figure around from this point on, partly because he turned out to have an illness that he may have had from childhood. At the age of 50 he was diagnosed with genetic haemochromatosis, an iron-overload disorder. This finally explained a lack of energy and not feeling well over many years, and led to several major health scares and interventions. It also meant there were some projects he could not proceed with or finish. Luckily he had all he needed at home, and it actually fitted in quite well with his preferred daily routine – up late in the morning, the afternoon nap, and late to bed. I've never known anyone to make so few concessions to his illness, although he did finally give up smoking. One has to comment on the amount of pharmaceuticals in their lives – they could have opened and run a field hospital in an African refugee camp. Congratulations to Sara and all the medical practitioners over the years who prolonged his life, and towards the end kept him amazingly free of pain, totally lucid, quite comfortable and in good spirits.

Johnny was quite relaxed about his 'legacy'. He knew he had accomplished valuable work which he had found extremely interesting, and despite his health, he achieved an enormous amount. He was modest about much of this, and felt privileged to have been given the opportunities. We did also discuss the different paradigms of how life can be lived and judged, and agreed that we didn't necessarily admire many of the so-called high achievers or leaders in the community.

His films – his main career vocation – are what he will be most remembered for, although he saw himself primarily as a poet. Documentaries such as *Lempad of Bali*, *Bali Triptych*, *Below the Wind* and *The Healing of Bali* won awards, were shown very widely internationally and were described variously as 'elegant', scholarly and beautiful', 'superbly crafted', 'stunning', 'the most innovative cinematographer', and so forth. When I told him I'd watched a particular film on a plane, he replied, 'Don't watch films on small screens!'

Johnny returned to Australia from Bali in 1988, and in 1990 he moved to Western Australia to lecture on Documentary and Media Production at Murdoch University for several years. As the many emails attest, he must have been an effective and admired teacher, and he was so understanding and approachable. He also more informally mentored many of us – from no doubt encouraging Toby into youth work and an awareness of social justice issues – to astutely steering me to the Faculty of Creative Arts at the University of Wollongong to do an MA.

When we were younger, we were very into astrology and the *I Ching* and so forth, and I brought with me to Perth information on Pisces, which was Johnny's zodiac sign. I thought it was a way of talking about that 'essence' I was going to have to describe at his funeral. Pisceans, apparently, 'understand that universal goals have greater meaning than personal ones' and Pisceans 'are able to communicate their high ideals and sense of purpose to others without condescension or elitist attitudes'. They are 'true believers'. They are also sensitive and shy, highly empathetic and compassionate.

We did discuss the statement that 'Pisces are the most highly evolved people of the zodiac'; but we did not discuss 'Pisceans teach us not to be afraid to let go of our earthly form, and that death is only the beginning of new life', although Johnny seemed to understand this intuitively.

Johnny commented that people were surprised he was so into sport. He played football well himself and was 'fleet of foot', even winning the marathon at Timbertop (Geelong Grammar's bush campus). He loved cricket deeply and we talked about the new guns in the Australian team, and Peter Roebuck's writing about cricket. Johnny thought he himself batted very classically, and his style has been described as 'elegant', which he rather hoped it was. He loved the Shane Warne era best.

Johnny adored books. I suspect he was buying them online right up to the last. His excuse, said with his naughty smile, was 'because of the dollar'. He read widely and deeply, and could summarise whatever he read for me very concisely. He was not heavy or dogmatic or boring with his information; he could be concise and light with serious and weighty ideas.

He assembled a very impressive library – primarily about Bali and Indonesia, and Aboriginal and Australian history. He had just finished reading most of Christopher Hitchens's essays in *Arguably*, which he thought was marvellous. Christopher in fact rang him on his last visit to Australia. He also dipped into Inga Clendinnen's Boyer lectures *True Stories* and we both admired her *Dancing with Strangers*. He loved Alex Miller's *Journey to the Stone Country* and *The Ancestor Game*, and told me I should read *The Glass Room* by Simon Mawer. Carole Muller's recent book *Bali Aga Villages: Field work in the 1980s* and a handsome new book on Walter Spies by Hans Rhodius were both handy on the coffee table. Johnny had co-authored the book *Walter Spies and Balinese Art* with Hans in 1980. Both books contained very grateful acknowledgements to John, and I wondered just how many other people he had helped with their research. He thought contemporary Balinese and Indonesian art was being overlooked internationally.

He loved poetry. Once when I rang he was listening to a recording of T.S. Eliot's *The Waste Land*. He had just finished reading a review of Joan Didion's *Blue Nights*, which he said contained hope as well as illness and death. I told him people were loving Booker Prize winner Julian Barnes's *The Sense of an Ending*. Within an hour or two Sara managed miraculously to get it delivered to their house, but by then he was really too ill to read it.

Over the last year or so we quite often discussed topics I was writing about on my blog, and he'd rein me in occasionally with remarks like 'you're sounding a bit fascist'. He thought the most pressing problem in the world was the growing disparity between the rich and poor. He described himself as a socialist – 'in the traditional meaning of the word'. He thought I should be reading George Soros on capitalism, and that it was particularly relevant to reread John Locke, the English philosopher, and Thomas Malthus, the English scholar.

We will each have our different memories of an extraordinary man who loved us as much and as easily as we loved him. He lived his life with such grace, and he faced his death with such dignity, and as tragic as it was, in those last weeks there were elements of great beauty.

Notes

1. The publication referred to here was *Lempad: The Illuminating Line*, a massive book produced by Puri Lukisan and Editions Didier Millet to function as a catalogue raisonné to the exhibition, held between 20 September and 20 October 2014. Chris Hill was a member of Murdoch University Art Board in 1993 and served as its Chair from 2007 to 2010. Sadly he died in 2014.
2. Probus is a global organisation of retired people.
3. *Bleaching Australia* was never made, but Johnny, with his sense of social justice, could see the irony of including the possible role of ancestors of some of the scions of Geelong Grammar School families during the 19th century in the oppression of Indigenous people in the Western District of Victoria.

A Reflection

Peter Gebhardt

I gave John his first teaching job. It was a decision made in fealty and rewarded a hundred times over by someone who was a natural teacher and for whom the students had a high regard, notwithstanding that their essays were often returned stained with his sherry, dry of course.

He had a vegetable plot at the bottom of All Saints College Bathurst, next to the Macquarie River – a sort of organic attempt before its time. There on Friday afternoons, students traipsed for 'Activities'. They loved him and his vegetation. He had a natural affinity with both the environment and with people.

He lived in a small, detached stucco shack behind Long House, a boarding house named after a bishop who was the father of Gavin Long, the Second World War historian.

His residence was a short distance from the piggery, where our children used to enjoy tripping from time to time. Johnny's room was as much a staging post as he was a bright and welcoming host. He was good with children, good with students and good for us anxiety-ridden adults. He was special, and it does us much good to recognise that. His life asks us to shelve pretension and hypocrisy, to live in what Samuel Johnson called 'the stability of truth'.

A Reflection

The journey to the garden took him past our 'Principal's Cottage', and cottage it was! On the way back he would drop in for a drink and space to smoke a cigarette with me in my smoking days. Johnny was too much harried about his smoking. It was part of his elegance and elan.

Johnny had a huge familial expectation to try to meet. He always loved his family. But he knew that he would have to transcend it to make his own completeness. He did so in a wonderful creative way: his Bali films are a complete testimony to that. He did so in his own way, with and in a spirit of a genuine regard for humanity. He loved his cricket. He loved the Geelong Football Club. He also loved the people who were the original owners of this land. That put him at odds with far too many of his contemporaries.

He wanted his old school to acknowledge, understand and accept the Western Districts' historical role in the attrition of Aboriginal people. I shared that hope with him and longed for something beyond a patronising gesture.

He had thrown off colonial shackles without abandoning the very strengths of the civilisation which had nurtured him.

There was a measure of honesty about Johnny which I truly loved and respected, a rare honesty. Understanding the long and scarifying history of his body's rebellion, we must accept that his love of nicotine may well have been more than an addiction or bad habit, just a pure necessity to enable him to offer his extraordinary gifts in a relative measure of comfort or discomfort.

What we should admire is his extraordinary courage in the face of every conceivable medical imbalance that can afflict a human being. Genetics play some cruel cards.

Fighting the battle that he had, he didn't have as much time as he deserved to demonstrate his gifts, his art and his craft, his skills and his conversations; but the time he did have, he used to the very best of what he had in store.

I realised some years ago that his 'tiredness' at Bathurst was an early symptom and sign. Hindsight doesn't help much, but he battled early and often to rise above the body's limitations. Smoking was a perfectly justifiable embodiment of stress and anxiety. We would all do well to avoid being hypocritical. He had to learn to suffer and to struggle in his own special way. He knew his habits were self-defeating but also self-exonerating. Such are the ambivalences which we all encounter on the journey.

Johnny was in the first class I ever taught. I don't know what he learned or if I taught him anything, but I do know the gifts of teaching and learning were sown then.

Growth is hazardous, but a few flowers blossomed and who could ask for anything more?

Johnny's friend was in that class. He was suddenly absent. Upon my enquiry, Johnny informed me, 'He has gone to get circumcised.' Such are the beauties of honesty and modern medicine!

After the courageous struggle, he needed some rest and that he has got. What he didn't get in an obvious way were the rewards he deserved. We, his friends, know better and acknowledge a beautiful life. The vegetables will continue to grow and the flowers blossom.

In the end, character, personality, independence and autonomy will win out against the currency of fat cheque books and corporate opulence. John lived and died in the spirit.

That is a triumph which trumps the obsession with possessions and the pursuit of power. It is much more restful. When Johnny was born in 1946, after three sisters, the flag was raised at Corio. Well, we

A Reflection

should all now raise another flag and one that reflects and manifests his loves from the past and his hopes for the future.

It would be a different flag. Johnny was a very modern man.

Part V

The Artist:
Poetry and Paintings

Introduction

Graeme MacRae

John had many interests and talents across many disciplines and media and a casual indifference to customary boundaries. Likewise his films are not easily categorised, spanning and combining conventions of genre, style and voice. Although it was as a filmmaker that he became known, John thought of himself, especially in his earlier years, primarily as a poet and even his filmmaking he saw in poetic terms: "It's all about your voice – in the poets sense – I've found it in poetry in its truest sense – occasionally in films."[1]

In his later years, when ill-health curtailed his filmmaking, he turned to painting. During his years in Canberra he had a view from his house to a nearby range of hills known as the Brindabellas. Later, in Melbourne he began a series of paintings of them – in shades of red/orange/yellow earth colours. Other paintings followed, mostly abstracted landscapes using Chinese inks and local ochres as well as acrylics.

While John took both his painting and also his poetry seriously, he made no claims about their artistic significance. A small sample of expert opinion concurs with this judgement, regarding them as the competent work of a gifted amateur. But, as many of his friends know, they are good to read and look at, and they offer insights into his thinking and his personal journey as an artist. A selection of them are reproduced here. John was also a good photographer and several of his photos are included with the images.

Note

1   From notes for a talk in a film workshop.

Notes from a Ricefield

Poems by John Darling, 1971–77

During this period, John was living full-time in Bali, in his simple bamboo and thatch *pondok* in the ricefields near Ubud. He was deeply absorbed in the natural and cultural beauty of Bali, but also in his own search for the meaning and path of his own life. His films were in the future, not even imagined, and poetry was the medium he chose for exploring and expressing his thoughts and feelings. Although he read widely, the form and style of his poems were influenced largely by those of the early Chinese Buddhist/Taoist hermit philosophers who also chose poetry as a medium of expression.

Translation of John Darling's poetry from English into Indonesian is by Isna Marifa.

John Darling

in the mountains	di gunung
i saw a river	kulihat sungai
running rapid.	mengalir deras.
for Buddha	untuk Sang Buddha
a deep pool	sendang yang dalam
ripples	air beriak
out from centre.	dari pusarnya.
in a quiet place	di tempat sunyi
a fat frog	katak tambun
croaks content	berdengkang puas
trapping his needs	menjerat hajatnya
from a flying world.	dari dunia beterbangan.

sometimes	ada kalanya
when alone	saat sendiri
visiting my melancholy,	bertamu dengan sendu
I feel another heart beating	kurasakan detak jantung lain
in some ill-defined distance.	tak jelas betul jaraknya.
I know	aku tahu
i have reaped	setumpuk ingatan manis
my own fond memories,	telah kutuai,
made them memories,	kujadikan kenangan,
I know	aku tahu
it is no use	tak guna
lamenting,	menyesal,
so usually	maka biasanya
I try to travel with a smile.	kucoba berkelana dengan senyuman.

Notes from a Ricefield

quiet	senyap
settling rain,	hujan mengendap,
slow drops from the eaves,	tetes perlahan dari tepian atap
through the trickling	di antara gemericik air
the birds still call of morning,	burung-burung pun menyambut pagi,
a puppy curls at my feet,	anak anjing meringkuk di kakiku,
and I think of you	dan aku memikirkan kamu
with work done	kerjaku tuntas
and time for rest and revel.	kini waktu rehat dan nikmat.

I like to live close to beauty,	aku senang hidup dekat keindahan,
now, surrounded by it, with	kini, dikelilingi olehnya,
no beauty in my heart.	indah tak ada di hatiku.

across	seberang
an eastern sea,	laut timur,
bright rising venus	bintang kejora terbit bersinar
beckons with a dawning beam.	memanggil dengan kilauan fajar.

the sounds of dawn	suara fajar
freshly exclude	segarnya menghapus
the memory of nights	memori malam
unseen busyness	keramaian tak terlihat
and exaggerated noise.	dan bahana berganda.

John Darling

a falling leaf
caught in morning's angled
   sun;
I thought it was a butterfly.

sehelai daun gugur
tertangkap sinar condong mentari
   pagi;
kukira seekor kupu-kupu.

what grace,
what style!
a chameleon surfs the wind
on a taro leaf.

wahai anggunnya,
wahai gayanya!
bunglon berselancar angin
di atas daun talas.

After the drabness
of a grey dawn
the sun rises
above dark eastern clouds
and glints on wet leaves.

Setelah kusamnya
fajar kelabu
mentari muncul
di atas awan gelap ufuk timur
dan kemilau pada daunan basah.

  Birds in joy
  sing praises
  of the unfolding day.

  Burung-burung ceria
  menyanyikan pujian pada
  hari yang menampakkan diri.

  Butterflies come
  (resplendent in new birth)
  to enjoy the sun.

  Kupu-kupu hadir
  (bersinar dalam kelahiran baru)
  nikmati sinar mentari.

Notes from a Ricefield

A broad-wing'd hazel butterfly flies a tricky path through a temple's banyan tree.	Kupu-kupu sayap lebar warna jerami terbang di alur rumit melalui beringinnya pura.

down by the river where I bathe, a long, green-glowing snake, (invisible at first in the young ferns), slowly, surely, climbed the vertical moss-dripped rock;	di pinggir sungai tempat aku mandi, seekor ular, panjang, hijau berpendar, (awalnya tak tampak di antara pakis muda), perlahan, pasti, menyelinap naik batuan curam, berteteskan lumut;

I would have thought it an
   impossible feat,
but such is the mastery of
   these primeval creatures.
	kiraku tak mungkin,
	namun begitulah trampilnya sang
	   makhluk purba.

hot and steamy comes the day, the grass hides furtive rustles as lizards enjoy the warmth	panas dan gerah hari tiba, rumput sembunyikan gemerisik senyap kadal menikmati kehangatan.

John Darling

In the sugar-cane	Di pokok tebu
a small yellow spine-bill	burung kuning mungil, penghisap madu
rustles the leaves in play.	bermain, menggerisik dedaunan.

here, in the hills	di sini, di bukit
where I live,	tempatku tinggal,
the wind arrives at midday;	angin datang tengah hari;
scattering the heat	hamburkan panas
in gentle ripples.	dengan alunan lembut.

a goat	seekor kambing
perched	bertengger
on a pile of rock	di tumpukan batu
surveys the world from a length	memindai buana dari panjangnya
of rope.	seutas tali.

A black snake,	Ular hitam,
its length entwined	tubuh melilit
rests, sunning	rehat, berjemur
on the temple step.	di tangga pura.

an auburn leaf	sehelai daun coklat kemerahan
rests on the jade cloister,	jeda pada beranda hijau lumut,
amid cooling ferns	di antara pakis-pakis menyejukkan
a river path winds down.	jalan setapak sungai turun berkelok.

Notes from a Ricefield

into the chasm of the flowing
   stream
falls a yellow bamboo leaf,
… held by some mysterious
   current
it gathers strength before it
   sails away …

ke dalam ngarai aliran sungai
sehelai daun bambu kuning jatuh
… ditopang suatu arus gaib
himpun daya sebelum berlayar
   jauh …

running
rippled dapples of sunlight
reflected on dark mossy rocks;
butterflies whisk between the
   creepers.

berlarian
kepingan sinar mentari mengalun
terpantul pada batuan berlumut kelam;
kupu-kupu terbang di antara tanaman
   rambat.

a glint of black/blue
on a butterfly's wing;
we are in space,
where is the stillness behind?

kilau hitam/biru
pada sayap kupu-kupu;
di ruang kita berada,
di mana hening bersembunyi?

hollow now
the chimes of cicadas:
in the forest
even leaves weep.

kini kopong
nyanyian sinayu
di dalam hutan
daunanpun menangis.

John Darling

in the still	dalam hening
before the storm	menjelang badai
a butterfly – hovers and lights	seekor kupu – melayang dan menjulang
– hovers and lights.	– melayang dan menjulang

a rush of wind,	sapuan angin,
shaken tresses	lambaian rambut tergerai
coconuts fall,	kelapa berjatuhan,
branches, even trees:	ranting, bahkan pohon:
rain follows-	diikuti hujan.

a small red flower	sekuntum bunga merah
wavers	bimbang
and holds	dan menanti
to the end of its long thin stem.	di ujung tangkai panjang pipih.

perched	bertengger
on the frangipani bough	di dahan pohon kamboja
a wagtail brusquely	burung pipit, gesit
waits out the rain.	menunggu redanya hujan.

after the rain	usai hujan
everywhere the sound	di mana-mana suara
of falling water;	air mengalir;
the padi-fields	bentangan sawah
a gurgling cascade.	riam gemericik.

Notes from a Ricefield

Not seen for a month,	tak tampak selama sebulan,
mount Agung*	Gunung Agung
steadfast	bertahan
after the heavy rain	selepas hujan lebat
reappears in azure majesty.	kembali muncul biru kemuliaan.

*Agung – (greatest), Gunung Agung (the great mountain) is the massive centrepiece of the landscape, the navel of the Balinese cosmos. Over 10,000 feet high, Agung last erupted in 1963.

a thin green snake	ular hijau pipih
crooked amongst the branches	berliku di antara ranting
rests in the drying sun.	rehat, berjemur di terik matahari

after a short glory	setelah kejayaan singkat
the withered hibiscus flower	kembang sepatu layu
hangs to the bush.	bergelayut pada semak.

the falling sun	matahari terbenam
behind the rain	di balik hujan
each heavy drop	tiap tetes berat
a glistening pearl.	mutiara berkilau.

John Darling

the palm leaf,
a kayon* in the wind;
the screen,
a rushing cloudscape.

daun palem,
seakan kayon di angin;
kelirnya,
bentangan awan bergegas.

* *Kayon – In wayang kulit (shadow puppet) performances the play is introduced and concluded by an intricate represenation of the holy banyan tree. It is the tree of life. Throughout a performance its dancing form plays many roles, an ascending soul, the gateway of heaven, it introduces the gods or a dawning day. It is a universal symbol.*

ants trek on a high bough;
amber silhouettes
before the setting sun.

semut berbaris di dahan tinggi
bayangan jingga
menyongsong terbenamnya matahari.

reds merge
layers of clouds to blues,
big birds high – silent
small birds whisper close,
moths flutter, frogs chant.

merah berbaur
lapisan awan menjadi biru,
burung besar tinggi – senyap
burung kecil berbisik dekat,
ngengat berdebar, katak berdendang.

shadowy mountains
a change of hues,
redder and deeper
stars unobserved welcome
    night.

pegunungan membayang
bergantian warna,
semakin merah dan dalam
bintang tak teramati menyambut
    malam.

Notes from a Ricefield

as evening comes　　　　　　saat sore tiba
spiders repair their webs　　　laba-laba merapikan sarangnya
in preparedness for night;　　bersiap untuk malam;
the time of light animals.　　saatnya para fauna halus.

the half moon's curious trace　　paruh-bulan penasaran
through glazed ricefields;　　　menelusuri pantulannya di sawah;
in search of pairing.　　　　　　mencari kembarnya.

a fish　　　　　seekor ikan
jumps　　　　　lompat
to the moon –　　ke bulan –
a sliver glint　　kilauan perak
as he　　　　　saat ia
twists　　　　　melingkar
and falls.　　　dan jatuh.

swelling　　　　　　　　　padat berisi
ears of rice　　　　　　　　bulir-bulir padi
stand silver in the moon　　tegak perak di sinar rembulan
above a swaying ocean.　　di atas laut bergelombang.

encircled　　　　　　　　　dikitari
by the moon,　　　　　　　rembulan,
the eagles glide　　　　　　rajawali melayang
in ghostly silhouettes.　　　dalam bayangan remang-remang.

John Darling

the full-moon
at dead of night
drops phosphorescence
on dewing fronds.

bulan purnama
di malam pekat
meneteskan pendar
pada dedaunan berembun.

rogs croak in the humid night
thunder rumbles
lightning
brightens the path home

katak berdengkang di malam gerah
geledek bersahutan
petir
menyinari jalan pulang.

what a welcome sight,
the warm glow
of the lamps of home;
in dark ricefields
a frog jumps!

pemandangan menyenangkan,
cahaya hangat
dari pelita di rumah;
di sawah gelap
seekor katak melompat!

fireflies
ignore the rain;
stars in the skyless night.

kunang-kunang
abaikan hujan;
bintang di malam tak berlangit.

in strokes of chinese ink;
the mountains drawn
across night's dark canvas.

usapan tinta cina;
gunung-gunung terlukis
di atas kanvas gelapnya malam.

Notes from a Ricefield

above passing storm clouds,   di atas awan badai berselang,
the rising moon;   terbit rembulan;
against western stars,   berlatar bintang di barat,
a white rainbow.   sebilah pelangi putih.

after the deafening rain;   usai hujan yang memekakkan;
listen to the silence   dengarkan heningnya
of happy frogs   katak-katak bahagia
and dripping trees.   dan pepohonan bertetesan.

swish…thump   desir…gedebuk
a palm leaf falls   daun palem jatuh
in the well-black dark;   di hitam-sumur kegelapan;
hesitantly,   ragu-ragu,
the frogs regain their chant.   para katak lanjutkan nyanyian.

how fragrant!   wah harumnya!
the echoes of gongs   gema suara gong
falling like dew,   berjatuhan bagai embun,
this white-moon night.   pada malam berbulan putih.

bright and sharp　　　　　　　cerah benderang
the still moonlit night;　　　　malam tenang bercahaya bulan;
only the high palms　　　　　hanya kelapa tinggi
whisper to a breeze.　　　　　yang berbisik pada bayu.

when the moon is strong　　　saat bulan cemerlang
and the sky clear　　　　　　dan langit bersih
great Agung* rests amongst　　Agung nan luhur bersandar di antara
　　the stars.　　　　　　　　　bintang.

*Agung – (greatest), Gunung Agung (the great mountain) is the massive centrepiece of the landscape, the navel of the Balinese cosmos. Over 10,000 feet high, Agung last erupted in 1963.

in twisted swirls　　　　　　　liak-liuk bergeliat
and liquid rivulets of　　　　　dan alunan cair suara berbisik,
　　whispered sounds,　　　　　pepohonan dan dedaunan
the trees and creeping foliage;　　　merambat;
far back　　　　　　　　　　jauh di belakang
solid in the moon…the　　　　kokoh di bawah kirana bulan…
　　mountain stands.　　　　　　gunung berdiri.

clear　　　　　　　　　　　　jelas
in a flash of lightning –　　　　saat kilatan petir –
Gunung Agung　　　　　　　Gunung Agung
(home of the gods).　　　　　(kediaman para dewa).

Notes from a Ricefield

the open lotus	teratai merekah
in the shadows of the moon,	di bawah bayangan rembulan,
bamboos	pohon bambu
stand silent	diam berdiri
in the breezeless night;	pada malam tak berbayu;
the quietness of familiar sounds	kelembutan suara-suara akrab
is broken by restless dogs.	terpecah oleh kawanan anjing resah.

the bamboo leaves	daunan bambu
are shadow drawings	adalah sketsa bayang-bayang
on the path,	di jalan setapak,
one full-moon night.	suatu malam bulan purnama.

reflection –	pantulan –
the yellowing moon	bulan menguning
falls below the palm-trees;	terbenam di balik pohon kelapa;
stars return	bintang-bintang kembali
to still-mirror'd rice fields.	pada sawah bercermin diam.

in darkness after the moon,	di kegelapan setelah bulan,
the small birds –	burung-burung kecil –
prophets of the morning.	utusan sang pagi.

John Darling

half-waning moon	bulan separuh pudar
at dawning day;	saat fajar menyingsing;
on a lotus cloud	di atas awan teratai
the stupa mountain rests.	terbujur gunung stupa.

after the passing moon;	setelah bulan berlalu;
bright dawning venus	bintang kejora bersinar terang
above the eastern sky.	di atas langit timur.

a branch	ranting
falls	luruh
on a windless night;	pada malam nirbayu;
a rot within chooses its moment.	lapuk di dalam memilih saatnya.

between	di sela-sela
the lilies of the pond,	rangkaian teratai di kolam,
images	bayangan
of moving sun and changing clouds,	mentari bergerak dan awan berarak,
from red misty mirror moments	dari saat cermin berkabut merah
of days arriving and departing	pertanda hari datang dan pergi
to bright midday zephyr flecked distortions.	menjadi siang terang bergurat distorsi angin sepoi.

Notes from a Ricefield

Warung

In reverie
I sit at the warung
sipping hot coffee.

children play
in the dust of the path,
cocks crow from their cages
a hen and her brood
gather given scraps;
the women
straight-backed
return heavy-loaded
(trussed baskets on their heads)
spreading the news of the
    market.

a sudden storm stops movement
people cluster
in familiar fellowship
under shelter
the hen huddles her chicks.

   a flamed course
--- a falling star ---
beautiful in its own destruction.

Warung

Melamun
aku duduk di warung
menyeruput kopi panas.

anak-anak bermain
di debunya jalan setapak,
ayam jago berkokok dari
    kandangnya
induk ayam dan anaknya
mengais sisa-sisa makanan;
perempuan
berpunggung tegak
kembali dengan beban berat
(keranjang di kepala, padat terikat)
menyebar kabar dari pasar.

badai tiba-tiba hentikan gerakan
orang berkumpul
dalam akrab persahabatan
berteduh
si induk ayam rangkul anak-anaknya.

jalur membara
--- bintang jatuh ---
indah dalam kehancuran diri.

John Darling

this poem	sajak ini
out of the shyness of my thoughts,	dari perenunganku yang malu-malu,
an upublished poet	penyair tanpa terbitan
driven by some force	didorong kekuatan
(that need	(suatu hasrat
that nothing satisfies but poetry)	tak terpuaskan kecuali oleh puisi)
not yet knowing	belum tahu
if I write for anybody	untuk siapa aku menulis
I await the verdict	menanti keputusan
for if I search a name	karena jika aku cari sebuah nama
it is with a child's feeling	dengan rasa tak acuh
of detachment –	seorang anak –
the child expected	anak yang diharapkan
but who feels he must ask to join the gang –	namun merasa harus diajak gabung dalam gerombolan –
lacking confidence of knowledge	rendah diri dengan ilmu
still shy and scared…	masih malu dan takut…
scared of not finding	takut tak menemukan
encouragement of a single path	dukungan terhadap jalur tunggal
for the single path of art is a great adventure.	karena jalur tunggal seni adalah petualangan besar.

head	kepala
down	menunduk
a long-beaked	penghisap-madu
honey-seeker	berparuh panjang
suckles	menetek
a hanging	bunga
scarlet	merah
flower.	menggelantung.

Notes from a Ricefield

the eyes
create the paths
before us.
we travel slowly,
taking by-ways,
pursuing images...
evening visions of red-eyed
  infinity
return reversed in dawn's
  embrace

mata
mencipta jalur
di hadapan kita.
kita melangkah perlahan,
mengambil jalan setapak,
berburu imaji...
pemandangan sore, merah-mata tak
  terhingga
kembali berbalik dalam pelukan
  fajar

above the blackening dusk
the mountain –
a golden flame;
a memory of the passing sun.

di atas senja menghitam
sang gunung –
lidah api keemasan;
mengenang mentari berselang.

in the still damp dawn
even bird calls are subdued;
stumbling for coffee
I stub my toe!

pada fajar lembab nan sepi
kicau burungpun redup;
sempoyong mencari kopi
jari kakiku terantuk!

enclosed by a bowl of stars;
to the west
the dark glaze cracks and
  grumbles.

diselubungi cawan bintang
ke arah barat
gelap kemilau berdentum dan
  menggerutu.

John Darling

Rain

Invisible,
I heard it
far away
in the windless dark.

a patter
on the leaves,
single
heavy drops,
and then
straight
down
it fell,
obliterating
other sounds of night.

welcome
by parched soil
this impregnation
releases
the savour
of conceiving seeds.

then,
in its extravagance,
overfilling
to find a river's course.

Hujan

Tak kasat mata,
terdengar
jauh
di kegelapan nirbayu.

rintik
pada dedaunan,
tetesan tunggal
berat,
kemudian
jatuh
langsung
ke bawah,
meniadakan
suara malam lainnya.

disambut
oleh tanah kerontang
penyemaian ini
melepas
aroma
benih-benih bunting.

lalu,
dengan limpah-ruah,
meluap
mencari aliran sebuah sungai.

John Darling Filmography

Bali Dream, 1983. **Consultant/Actor**.
   Directed by Istvan Szabo. ZDF
Bali Hash, 1989. **Co-Producer/Co-Director** (with John Moyle).
   Taman Sari Productions Pty Ltd.
Bali Triptych, 1987. **Writer/Director/Location Producer**.
   Documentary series: I – Between the Mountain and the Sea; II – The Path of the Soul; III – Demons and Deities. Ronin Films.
Beauty and Riches, 1980. **Consultant**.
   Documentary. IKON TV/SBS TV.
Below the Wind, 1993–94. **Writer/Director**.
   Produced by Andrew Ogilvie. Electric Pictures Pty Ltd.
Birthrites, 2002. **Consultant**.
   Produced and directed by Jennifer Gherardi. Jag Films.
A Day in the Life of a Child – Bali, 1989. **Consultant**.
   Produced and directed by Jacquie Sykes. ABC TV/UNICEF.
The Healing of Bali, 2003. **Writer/Director**.
   Produced by John Darling and Sara Darling.
The Human Face of Indonesia, 1984. **Consultant/Researcher**.
   Produced by Rob McAuley. Film Australia. Documentary series. Episode 'Master of the Shadows' written and directed by John Darling.
The Human Race, 1982. **Consultant**.
   Presented by Desmond Morris. ITV Television, England.
Lempad of Bali, 1980. **Producer/Co-Director** (with Lorne Blair).
   Australian Broadcasting Commission / Australian National University.
Quest for Healing. **Consultant**.
   Produced by Richard Davis. Independent Productions Sydney.
Slowboat from Surabaya, 1988. **Location Producer**.
   Documentary series. Episode 'Five Faces of God' produced and directed by John Darling. Phillip Emanuel Productions Ltd.
Winds of Change, 1997–98. **Consultant**.
   Produced by Andrew Ogilvie and Alan Carter, directed by Alan Carter. Alley Kat Productions Pty Ltd/Electric Pictures Pty Ltd.

Supervised Student Productions

Across A Silent Land, 1996. **Executive Producer/Supervisor**.
>Producer/Director: Vicki Biorac. Submission for Honours in Screen Production at the School of Humanities, Murdoch University.

Choice Funerals, 1997. **Executive Producer/Supervisor**.
>Producer/Director: Jennifer Gherardi. Submission for Honours in Screen Production at the School of Humanities, Murdoch University.

Golden Mile 1995. **Executive Producer/Supervisor**.
>Produced and directed by John Lang. Honours project, Communication Studies, Murdoch University.

Contributors

Ace Bourke is one of Australia's leading independent art curators and is an Aboriginal Art and colonial art specialist. He and John became friends when they were studying at the Australian National University in the 1960s.

Bruce Carpenter has lived in Bali since the early 1970s. Inspired by Indonesian and Balinese art, he has authored and co-authored more than 20 books and scores of articles on the archipelago's art, history and culture including co-ordinating and editing the definitive book about I Gusti Nyoman Lempad, *Lempad: the illuminating Line*. He got to know John during their time in Ubud in the 1970s and through their mutual friendship with Lempad's son I Gusti Made Sumung.

Diana Darling is a freelance writer and editor who has been living in Bali since 1980. She was married to John Darling from 1981 to 1987.

James Darling, not related to John, went to the same school. They played cricket together and were close friends for more than 50 years. James is now a farmer, environmentalist, writer and artist. He lives in rural South Australia.

Sara Darling trained as a nurse, operated several small businesses and graduated from Murdoch University. In 1990 she met John and collaborated with him on two major documentaries and they married soon afterwards. After his death she initiated the John Darling Fellowship for an exchange of Australian and Indonesian documentary filmmakers. Currently, she is a special education teacher working with students with learning difficulties.

Peter Gebhardt (1936–2017), headmaster, county court judge and published poet, went to Geelong Grammar School where he was taught by John's father. He arranged a teaching position for John when he returned from Bali, at Bathurst Grammar School while he was headmaster there. They saw themselves as kindred spirits.

Duncan Graham has been a journalist for more than 40 years in print, radio and TV. He is the author of *People Next Door* (UWA Press) and winner of the Walkley Award and Human Rights awards. He is now writing for the English-language media in Indonesia from within Indonesia. He knew John and reviewed most of his films.

David Hanan taught Film Studies at Monash University for many years and is currently an honorary fellow at the Asia Institute, University of Melbourne. He also set up links between the Indonesian film world and Australian film festivals and filmmakers, and has been involved in Indonesian film subtitle translations and film preservation projects.

Contributors

Rio Helmi is a well-known Indonesian photographer who has lived for many years in Ubud. His photographs have been published in numerous books, and he is the creator of the blog 'Ubud Now and Then'. He was a close friend of John Darling, especially during the years John lived in Bali.

Chris Hill (1944–2014) was good friend of John Darling. They met at Murchdoch University, where Chris was member of Murdoch University Art Board in 1993, and its Chair from 2007 to 2010.

Tjokorde Gede Mahatma Putra Kerthyasa is a member of the leading noble family of Ubud and a natural healer by profession. John was close to his parents and the whole family in Ubud, and also when the family lived in Sydney during the 1990s.

E. Douglas Lewis is an anthropologist who has been researching in Flores for 50 years. He taught at the University of Melbourne for 20 years and is now an Adjunct Professor in Global Studies at RMIT University and Senior Research Associate at the Centre for Research on Religion and Culture in Maumere, Flores. He has published two books and many articles on his research in Flores as well as a film (with Timothy and Patsy Asch) *A Celebration of Origins* (1993) and a book about ethnographic film.

Anton Lucas is an Adjunct Associate Professor in the College of Humanities and Social Sciences at Flinders University, South Australia. His publications include books and articles on the

Indonesian revolution, and on agrarian and environmental issues. His connection with John goes back to their schooldays together, and they began their research careers in Indonesia at the same time in 1970.

Graeme MacRae is an anthropologist who works at Massey University, Auckland. He has been researching in Indonesia, mainly Bali, since the early 1990s. His connection with John was originally through the same neighbourhood, family and mentor that John had lived with two decades earlier.

Toby Miller is a British/Australian-American interdisciplinary social scientist whose areas of concentration include cultural studies and media studies. He was chair of the Department of Media & Cultural Studies at the University of California, Riverside (UCR) and is most recently a professor at Loughborough University. He was a student, then colleague of John Darling at Murdoch University in the 1990s.

Thomas Reuter is a former professor and current Professorial Fellow at the Asia Institute of the University of Melbourne and a trustee of the World Academy of Arts and Science, and fellow of two European Academies. He has been researching in Bali and Java since the early 1990s, and has published more than 150 articles and 15 books on a wide range of topics, as well as making a film, *The Java Spirit*. He worked with John Darling as a cultural advisor on John's final film, *The Healing of Bali*.

Contributors

Made Wijaya (1953–2016) was born Michael White in Australia. He was adopted into a Balinese Brahmin family in 1973 and was initiated Made Wijaya by a Balinese priest. He became a successful landscape designer and a notorious diarist and satirist. He is best known as an uncanny observer of Balinese society, and he created hundreds of informal videos of Balinese ritual. Made and John were very close friends, especially in the 1970s.

Peronelle Windeyer is the daughter of HB (Barney) Hutton, who was a teacher at Geelong Grammar, and she lived at the school. She was six years older than John and watched him grow up. There were close connections between the Hutton and Darling families. She is therefore well placed to provide rare independent insight into John's early life.